List of Contents

Introduction: Unveiling the Map of Dreams

Every one of us has a dream—a shimmering vision of the life we long to lead, the person we aspire to become, the accomplishments we yearn to achieve. These dreams take root within us, igniting a fire of possibility and potential. They're the whispers of our heart, the echoes of our deepest desires. And yet, all too often, they remain elusive, hidden behind a veil of doubt, fear, and uncertainty

But here's the thing: the journey to realizing our dreams isn't a straight, unbroken road. It's not a mere checklist of tasks or a linear progression from point A to point B. No, it's a multidimensional expedition, a journey that demands self-discovery, resilience, and a fearless embrace of change. It's a journey that requires a map—a map that will guide us through uncharted territories, help us navigate storms, and lead us to the treasures that await.

This book is that map. It's your compass, your guiding light, your unwavering companion on this odyssey towards the life you've envisioned. But unlike traditional maps, this one doesn't outline territories or landmarks; instead, it traces the contours of your mind, the landscape of your emotions, and the architecture of your beliefs.

As we embark on this journey together, you'll discover that achieving your dreams isn't solely about checking off a to-do list. It's about a profound transformation—an evolution of your mindset, a renewal of your spirit, and a recalibration of your habits. It's about turning those sparks of inspiration into the fuel that propels you forward, even when the path seems steep and uncertain.

Throughout the chapters that follow, we'll delve into the inner workings of dream achievement. We'll dive into the intricacies of setting intentions, embracing failures, and building unshakable self-confidence. We'll explore the power of visualization and the magic of consistent action. But this journey is not just about reaching the destination; it's about savoring each step along the way.

It's easy to become entangled in the complexities of daily life, to lose sight of the dreams that once burned brightly within us. We get caught up in the mundane, distracted by the urgent, and before we know it, our dreams are relegated to the shadows. But fear not, for within these pages, you'll find the tools to rekindle those flames, to stoke the fires of your passion, and to create a life that reflects your authentic desires.

The chapters that lie ahead are a treasure trove of insights, strategies, and wisdom garnered from the experiences of dreamers who've come before you. They're a compilation of proven principles and cutting-edge concepts that will help you unravel the mysteries of your potential. But remember, dear reader, this book is not a one-size-fits-all manual. It's a collection of possibilities, a framework of ideas that you can unite into your own unique journey.

And as we embark upon this expedition together, I encourage you to approach each chapter with an open heart and a curious mind. Reflect on the concepts, apply them to your own life, and allow them to shape your perspective. Your dreams are the raw material; this book is the chisel that will help you sculpt them into reality.

So, let us set forth on this adventure—a journey of introspection, growth, and ultimate fulfillment. Let this book be your guide, your confidant, and your source of inspiration. As you turn the pages, remember that you're not alone on this path. You are part of a vast community of dreamers, all connected by the shared aspiration to create lives of purpose, joy, and achievement.

The map is before you, the pen is in your hand, and the unwritten chapters of your life are waiting to be authored. Let's begin this journey of transformation, one word at a time, one insight at a time. Together, we'll uncover the secrets to unlocking your potential, embracing your dreams, and crafting a life that resonates with your deepest desires.

Chapter 1: Introduction to Dream Achievement

Understanding the Power of Dreams

In the boundless realm of human experience, one force has the remarkable ability to stir our souls, ignite our ambitions, and guide us through life's labyrinthine journey: dreams. Picture them as beacons of light piercing through the fog of uncertainty, as the threads that weave the fabric of our aspirations, as the whispers of destiny calling us to action.

Dreams as a Source of Motivation

Dreams, those vivid mental sketches of a future we yearn for, are the very wellspring of motivation. They are the fire that fuels our every step, igniting the passion that propels us beyond our comfort zones. But what gives dreams this profound influence? It's the magic of possibility.

Consider the ardent inventor, envisioning a world transformed by their innovation. Or the athlete, imagining the roar of the crowd as they cross the finish line. These dreams are catalysts, pulling us forward, urging us to push harder and reach higher. Dreams stoke the flames of ambition, turning mere potential into kinetic action.

A dream is more than a whimsical fantasy; it's an architect's blueprint for a better life. It lays the foundation for tangible goals, fostering a connection between the ethereal and the concrete. And as we nurture and feed these dreams, they

reciprocate by energizing us in ways we never thought
possible.

The Impact of Achieving Dreams

Imagine standing at the precipice of accomplishment,
surveying the landscape of your achievements. That view,
my friend, is nothing short of exhilarating. The impact of
achieving dreams extends far beyond the individual; it
resonates in the lives you touch and the world you
influence.

When you achieve a dream, you become a living testament
to human potential. You inspire others to chase their
aspirations, to conquer their fears, to transform mere
existence into a life rich with purpose. Dreams actualized
are like ripples in a pond, radiating positivity outward and
touching the lives of those who witness your journey.

Think about the joy that bubbles forth when you realize
you've turned the once-impossible into your own personal
reality. This joy, this triumph, is infectious, spurring you to
pursue even grander dreams and setting a precedent for
embracing challenges head-on.

Overcoming Doubts and Skepticism

Yet, the path to dream achievement isn't always lined with
rose petals. Doubts and skepticism, those naysayers of
possibility, often rear their heads. They cast shadows on the
brilliance of our dreams, whispering insidious notions of
"impractical" or "unattainable."

Navigating the terrain of doubt is a formidable task, but it's a crucial part of the journey. Doubts serve as mirrors, reflecting the insecurities within us. They demand introspection and self-assessment: Are our dreams truly aligned with our values? Are we prepared to face and address the obstacles in our path?

Remember, the most audacious dreams are the ones that defy conventional wisdom. Skepticism is but a stepping stone toward achieving them. It's an invitation to fortify our resolve, to fine-tune our strategies, and to seek out those who have walked the path before us. Doubt is not a stop sign; it's a checkpoint that invites us to reaffirm our commitment to the dreams that pulse within us.

Dreams are more than whimsical musings; they are the very essence of human potential. They have the power to ignite motivation, amplify impact, and guide us through the labyrinth of doubt. As we journey together through the chapters ahead, remember that within your dreams lies the map to the life you're meant to live. Embrace them, nurture them, and watch as they unfold into a reality beyond your wildest imagination.

The Psychology of Dream Setting

In the vast expanse of our lives, dreams serve as the guiding stars that illuminate our paths, beckoning us to embark on remarkable journeys of self-discovery and achievement. It's within this luminous realm of dreams that we uncover the boundless potential that resides within us—potential that is often obscured by the mundane routines of everyday life. Welcome to a chapter that delves into the very heart of dream achievement, exploring the intricate psychology that shapes our aspirations and fuels our determination to turn these dreams into reality.

The Role of Vision in Dream Achievement
Imagine a world without vision—a realm devoid of the ability to imagine, conceptualize, and visualize. Without this fundamental capacity, our dreams would remain trapped in the recesses of our minds, forever concealed from the light of day. Vision is the architect of our dreams, the artist that paints the canvas of our future with vibrant strokes of possibility. When we craft a vision of our dreams, we create a roadmap that charts our course and guides our actions.

Envision your dreams as a lighthouse that guides your ship through the stormy seas of life. This beacon of light cuts through the darkness, providing clarity and direction even in the midst of uncertainty. As you craft your vision, allow your imagination to run free—see, feel, and experience the very essence of your dream coming to fruition. This vivid mental imagery fuels your motivation, transforming your dream from a mere abstraction into a tangible reality that you can almost touch.

Setting Realistic and Ambitious Dreams

The journey of dream achievement is a delicate balance between setting aspirations that stretch your capabilities and grounding them in reality. Setting dreams that are too far-fetched may lead to frustration and disillusionment, while aiming too low can stifle your potential and limit your growth. The key lies in crafting dreams that inspire you to rise to new heights while also being achievable with dedication and effort.

Consider this process as planting a seed. Just as a seed requires the right amount of water, sunlight, and nurturing to blossom, your dreams need the right mix of inspiration, effort, and action. Choose dreams that resonate with your passions and align with your strengths. Then, break these dreams into smaller, manageable goals that pave the way to their realization. This step-by-step approach not only propels you forward but also instills a sense of accomplishment with each milestone you achieve.

Identifying Personal Values and Dreams

The heart of dream achievement is deeply intertwined with your core values. Think of your values as the compass that guides your decisions and actions. When your dreams are in harmony with your values, you forge a powerful connection that propels you forward even in the face of challenges. To identify your values, reflect on what truly matters to you, what gives your life meaning, and what you're willing to dedicate your time and effort to.

Imagine your values as the roots of a magnificent tree, grounding you and providing stability as you reach for the skies. As you identify your values, allow them to infuse your dreams with purpose and significance. Ask yourself: How do my dreams align with what I hold dear? How can my aspirations contribute not only to my personal growth but also to the betterment of the world around me?

The psychology of dream setting is an intricate dance between envisioning the future, crafting dreams that balance ambition and realism, and aligning these dreams with your core values. This sub chapter has merely scratched the surface of this profound topic. By understanding the role of vision, setting realistic yet ambitious dreams, and identifying your personal values, you've taken the first steps toward a transformative journey of dream achievement. As we continue our exploration, you'll uncover more insights and tools to propel you toward the fulfillment of your most cherished dreams.

The Connection Between Dreams and Actions
Dreams have an enchanting quality, don't they? They're like windows to our desires, revealing the splendid framework of our aspirations. But there's a bridge that links those dreams to reality, and that bridge is called action. Welcome to the transformative realm where your dreams are brought to life through the power of action – a realm where your

visions become tangible and your aspirations become achievements.

Turning Dreams into Concrete Goals

Imagine having a treasure map, one that guides you step by step towards your most cherished dreams. This map is created by turning your dreams into concrete goals. Goals provide the blueprint, the strategic plan, the roadmap that takes your fanciful dreams and translates them into actionable steps. They give your dreams structure, breaking them down into manageable parts that are less daunting and more achievable.

To do this, start by defining your dreams with clarity. What exactly do you want to achieve? Be specific. Whether it's starting your own business, writing a book, traveling the world, or mastering a new skill, the more precisely you define your dream, the more vividly it will come to life.

Next, break down your dream into smaller, measurable goals. If your dream is to write a book, for instance, your goals could include completing a certain number of chapters within a given timeframe. These smaller goals become milestones that not only help you measure your progress but also maintain your motivation as you tick them off, one by one.

The Importance of Taking Consistent Action

Setting goals is like planting seeds, and taking consistent action is how you water and nurture those seeds. It's the act of showing up day after day, dedicating time and effort, and moving steadily toward your goals. Consistency is the fuel that propels your dreams forward.

Think of it as a savings account for your dreams. Every action you take, no matter how small, contributes to the overall growth. Each sentence you write for your book, each product idea you develop, each language lesson you complete – they're all deposits into the account of your aspirations. And over time, these deposits accumulate, compounding into substantial progress.

Overcoming Procrastination and Fear
Procrastination and fear are two formidable foes that can hinder your journey from dreams to reality. They often form a seemingly impenetrable barrier between you and your goals. But fear not; they can be conquered.

Procrastination is like a sly thief that steals your time and productivity. It feeds on uncertainty and lack of focus. To combat it, break your goals into even smaller tasks. This reduces the intimidation factor, making it easier to start. Set deadlines for these tasks and create a reward system for when you complete them. Before you know it, you'll have momentum on your side.

Fear, on the other hand, often disguises itself as caution. It whispers doubts and worst-case scenarios in your ear. But remember, fear is just a mental construct – it's not real. Counteract it with positive self-talk and visualization. Imagine yourself succeeding, imagine the joy of accomplishing your goals, and gradually, fear will lose its grip.

Taking that first step can be daunting, but action is the antidote to fear. Each action you take weakens fear's hold, making room for confidence to flourish.

In the grand journey of achieving dreams, action is the thread that weaves through each moment, each endeavor. It's the force that turns mere wishes into concrete achievements. Your dreams are the stars; your actions are the constellations. As you move forward, remember that the journey is just as enchanting as the destination. So, embrace it fully, and let your actions paint the canvas of your dreams with vibrant, resplendent hues.

Chapter 2: Cultivating the Right Mindset

The Power of a Positive Mindset

In the journey towards achieving our dreams, our mindset stands as the foundation upon which everything is built. It's the driving force that propels us forward, or it's the anchor that holds us back. A positive mindset isn't just a fluffy catchphrase; it's a powerful tool that shapes the reality we experience. Let's delve into the transformative power of cultivating a positive mindset and how it can profoundly impact our pursuit of dream achievement.

Shifting from Limiting Beliefs to Empowering Beliefs

Imagine your mind as a garden. The seeds you plant are your beliefs. Limiting beliefs are like weeds that hinder growth, while empowering beliefs are like nurturing soil that allows your dreams to flourish. These beliefs, often ingrained in us since childhood, shape our perception of what's possible.

It's crucial to identify and challenge those limiting beliefs. Ask yourself, "What beliefs are holding me back?" Are you telling yourself you're not skilled enough, not worthy of success, or that dreams are for others, not you? These beliefs are not facts; they're assumptions. Challenge them with evidence to the contrary. Replace them with empowering beliefs that affirm your potential: "I can learn and grow," "I am capable of achieving great things," and "Dreams are within my reach."

Embracing a Growth Mindset for Dream Achievement
One of the most profound shifts you can make is adopting a growth mindset. Coined by psychologist Carol Dweck, a growth mindset is the belief that abilities and intelligence can be developed through effort and learning. It's about embracing challenges, persisting in the face of setbacks, and seeing failures as stepping stones to success.

Imagine a child learning to ride a bike. If they give up after falling a few times, they'll never learn. But with a growth mindset, they keep trying, learning from their mistakes, and eventually riding confidently. Similarly, in your pursuit of dreams, setbacks are opportunities to learn and improve. Embrace challenges as chances to develop your skills and resilience. Your mindset can turn stumbling blocks into stepping stones.

Using Affirmations to Shape Your Mindset
Affirmations are like a daily mental workout for your mindset. They're positive statements that help rewire your thinking patterns. Repeating affirmations daily can gradually replace negative self-talk with empowering beliefs.

Craft your affirmations to be present, positive, and personal. For example, if your dream is to become a successful author, your affirmation might be: "I am a talented and successful author, and my words have a positive impact on others." Repeat these affirmations consistently, especially during moments of self-doubt.

Remember, a positive mindset isn't about ignoring challenges or wearing rose-colored glasses. It's about facing challenges with a belief that you can overcome them. Henry Ford famously said, "Whether you think you can or you think you can't, you're right." Your mindset shapes your actions, and your actions shape your reality.

As you cultivate a positive mindset, notice how your thoughts, emotions, and behaviors align with your dreams. The journey to dream achievement isn't always smooth, but a positive mindset equips you with the resilience, creativity, and determination to overcome obstacles. It's about rewiring your mind to see opportunities where you once saw roadblocks. In the vast landscape of your dreams, your mindset is the compass that guides you toward success.

Building Self-Confidence and Self-Efficacy

In the intricate journey of achieving your dreams, there exists a vital cornerstone that forms the bedrock of success: self-confidence and self-efficacy. These two pillars aren't mere buzzwords; they're the potent elixirs that fuel your drive and determination to make your dreams a reality. In this sub-chapter, we'll delve deep into the art of cultivating unshakable self-confidence and fostering unwavering self-efficacy, arming you with the tools you need to overcome challenges and stride confidently towards your aspirations.

Recognizing Your Strengths and Accomplishments

Imagine standing before a mirror that reflects not just your outer appearance, but the dazzling array of strengths and achievements that have shaped you. Often, we're so immersed in the currents of our daily lives that we fail to recognize the gems within us. Take a moment to reflect on your journey – those moments of triumph, big and small, that have sculpted you. Recognizing your strengths doesn't entail boasting; it's about acknowledging the qualities that have propelled you forward.

Every step you've taken, every hurdle you've overcome, has contributed to the person you are today. Harnessing this awareness boosts your self-image, instilling a newfound belief in your capabilities. From navigating complex tasks to overcoming personal struggles, these are your badges of honor that deserve to be celebrated.

Embracing Failures as Learning Opportunities

Failure is a word that often carries a heavy weight, laden with negative connotations. However, the path to success is often paved with failures that are less like roadblocks and more like stepping stones. When you shift your perspective and view failure as a powerful teacher, the narrative changes. It's not about avoiding failure; it's about learning from it.

Each setback is a classroom where life imparts invaluable lessons. Think of Thomas Edison, who faced countless failures before creating the light bulb. His response to his 'failures'? "I have not failed. I've just found 10,000 ways that won't work." That's the spirit. Embrace failures, dissect them, understand their anatomy, and turn them into stepping stones towards progress. This mindset shift enhances self-efficacy – your belief in your capacity to influence the outcome.

Cultivating Unshakeable Self-Confidence

Now, let's journey to the heart of unshakeable self-confidence. Picture it as a tree – its roots deeply anchored in self-awareness and acceptance, its branches reaching out towards the skies of endless possibilities. To cultivate this tree, we must first nurture our self-worth. Your worth isn't determined by external validation; it's intrinsic and unchangeable. Remind yourself of your uniqueness, your talents, and your potential.

The framework of self-confidence is woven with the threads of positive self-talk. When challenges arise, pause and reframe your inner dialogue. Replace self-doubt with affirmations that reflect your capabilities. As Marisa Peer puts it, "You are enough." Embrace this mantra, for it forms the foundation of your unshakeable self-confidence.

However, even the most confident individuals face storms of self-doubt. The key is acknowledging these doubts without letting them define you. This acknowledgment fuels your resilience, reminding you that it's okay to feel uncertain sometimes. Remember, confidence isn't a destination; it's a journey of growth and self-discovery.

In the journey of achieving your dreams, self-confidence and self-efficacy are the vibrant threads that bring the image into focus. By recognizing your strengths, embracing failures as stepping stones, and cultivating unshakable self-confidence, you're not merely preparing for success – you're embodying it. You're staking your claim in the landscape of your dreams, guided by the unwavering compass of belief in yourself.

Overcoming Obstacles and Challenges

In the grand journey of realizing our dreams, obstacles and challenges are as certain as the sunrise. They are the tests that make our dreams worth pursuing, the trials that shape us into who we need to be to reach those distant horizons. The path to success is not a perfectly paved highway, but rather a rugged trail through the wilderness, fraught with setbacks and roadblocks. In this sub-chapter, we delve into the art of overcoming these very challenges and cultivating the resilience required to stay the course.

Developing Resilience in the Face of Setbacks

Resilience, that elusive yet indispensable trait, is what separates those who merely dream from those who triumphantly achieve. Resilience is not the absence of challenges; it's the ability to bounce back from them. When we encounter setbacks – the missed opportunities, the unexpected failures – we have a choice: to crumble under their weight or to rise stronger.

Resilience begins with a mindset shift. Instead of viewing setbacks as dead ends, we can reframe them as detours – alternate routes that lead us to unexpected, yet potentially even better destinations. This shift in perspective empowers us to view challenges not as roadblocks, but as stepping stones. Each obstacle is a chance to learn, to adapt, and to grow.

Problem-Solving Strategies for Dream Obstacles
The art of problem-solving is a cornerstone of navigating life's challenges. It's about approaching obstacles with a sense of curiosity and a determination to find solutions. When faced with a seemingly insurmountable challenge, break it down into smaller, manageable components. Ask yourself: What can I tackle first? What resources can I leverage? Who can I seek guidance from?

Moreover, consider the power of creative thinking. The most innovative solutions often arise from looking at a problem through a different lens. This might mean borrowing insights from other fields or inviting diverse perspectives into the discussion. Embrace trial and error, and understand that failures are but experiments on the path to success.

Seeking Support and Collaboration

Navigating challenges doesn't have to be a solitary endeavor. In fact, seeking support and collaboration can amplify our resilience and accelerate our progress. We're not meant to have all the answers or to shoulder every burden alone. Reach out to mentors, peers, or friends who can offer guidance or a fresh perspective.

Collaboration, too, is a formidable tool in overcoming obstacles. Sometimes, the very challenge we face is one that someone else has already conquered. Collaborative efforts bring together a group of talents and experiences, creating a safety net of shared wisdom. A supportive community can provide encouragement during moments of doubt and act as a sounding board for your ideas.

In the journey toward your dreams, remember that setbacks and challenges are not signs to turn back but signals to forge ahead with greater determination. Embrace resilience as your companion, problem-solving as your strategy, and support as your safety net. Through this, you'll not only overcome challenges but transcend them, emerging with a deeper understanding of yourself and an unshakable belief in your ability to conquer whatever lies ahead.

Chapter 3: Visualization and Manifestation

The Art of Creative Visualization

In the journey of achieving our dreams, the power of the mind cannot be underestimated. It's the canvas upon which our aspirations take shape, the launching pad for our ambitions. This is where the art of creative visualization comes into play—a technique that transcends mere wishful thinking and transforms it into a powerful tool for manifesting our deepest desires.

Using Imagination to Envision Dream Success

At its core, creative visualization is a mental practice that involves imagining yourself in a future state of accomplishment. It's the act of vividly picturing your goals as already achieved, allowing your mind to delve into the realm of possibilities without the constraints of your current reality. When you close your eyes and visualize your success, you're creating a bridge between your present circumstances and the life you envision.

Start by choosing a quiet space where you won't be interrupted. Close your eyes, take a few deep breaths, and allow yourself to relax. Then, visualize your dream in intricate detail. Imagine the surroundings, the people, the sights, and even the sounds. If your dream is to speak on a stage, picture the lights shining down on you, the crowd's anticipation, and the sensation of confidence surging through your veins. The more vivid your imagination, the more potent the effects of visualization become.

Incorporating Senses for Vivid Visualization

But here's where creative visualization takes an even more fascinating turn: it's not just about seeing the images in your mind. Engage all your senses to make the experience richer and more real. Feel the texture of the stage under your feet, hear the applause, sense the adrenaline coursing through your body. The mind doesn't distinguish between what's real and what's vividly imagined, so the more senses you involve, the more authentic the experience becomes.

This multisensory approach to visualization enhances the neural connections in your brain, effectively training it to believe in the possibility of your dreams. When your brain becomes familiar with these imagined scenarios, it starts paving the way for turning them into reality. It's like rehearsing for your success in the theater of your mind before stepping onto the stage of life.

Aligning Emotions with Visualized Outcomes

Now, let's delve into a crucial element of creative visualization: emotion. It's not enough to visualize your dreams mechanically; you must infuse them with genuine emotion. Feel the joy, the pride, the satisfaction as if you've already achieved your goals. When you align positive emotions with your visualizations, you create a powerful synergy that sends a clear message to your subconscious mind: "This is what I desire, and I believe in it wholeheartedly."

Think about a time when you achieved something significant. Recall the emotions you felt—perhaps excitement, relief, or even a sense of accomplishment. By evoking these emotions during your visualization practice, you're telling your brain that this achievement is not just a far-off possibility; it's an imminent reality.

Incorporating emotions into your visualization practice also helps to eliminate doubts and fears. When you're immersed in positive feelings associated with your dreams, negative thoughts struggle to find a foothold. You're essentially rewiring your brain to focus on the positive aspects and discard the self-doubt that often holds us back.

The art of creative visualization is a remarkable technique that allows you to step into the shoes of your future self, experiencing success before it happens. By employing all your senses and imbuing your visualizations with genuine emotions, you're crafting a detailed roadmap to guide you towards your dreams. Remember, what you consistently visualize and believe, you ultimately manifest. So, let your imagination run wild, your senses come alive, and your heart resonate with the success that's within your grasp.

Law of Attraction and Manifestation

In the history of human experience, the Law of Attraction stands as a thread that weaves together the realms of thought, intention, and reality. This concept, often heralded as one of the cornerstones of personal transformation and success, invites us to explore the profound interconnectedness between our inner world and the external universe. In this exploration, we uncover the intricate dance of energies that shape the path to our dreams.

Understanding the Basics of the Law of Attraction

At its essence, the Law of Attraction is a reflection of the age-old adage "like attracts like." This law proposes that the energy vibrations we emit through our thoughts, emotions, and beliefs resonate with corresponding energies in the universe, leading to the manifestation of experiences that align with our predominant mental states. In essence, the thoughts we harbor act as magnets, drawing into our lives events, people, and circumstances that mirror our internal frequencies.

While the idea might appear simple, its implications are profound. Imagine your mind as a radio transmitter, constantly sending out signals into the ether. These signals, whether positive or negative, are the blueprints that shape the experiences you attract. If your mental landscape is dominated by positivity and belief in your dreams, the universe responds in kind, opening doors and clearing pathways. Conversely, dwelling on doubts and fears can inadvertently attract situations that reinforce those very doubts.

Setting Clear Intentions for Manifestation

Intentions act as the compass that guides the ship of the Law of Attraction. They are the deliberate declarations of what you wish to bring into your life, signposts that direct the universe's attention to your deepest desires. Yet, setting intentions goes beyond simply stating your wishes; it involves a profound connection between your heart and mind.

To set intentions effectively, you must embark on a journey of self-discovery. What do you truly yearn for? What ignites the fire within you? Answering these questions helps crystallize your aspirations into clear, focused intentions. For instance, if your dream is to establish a thriving business, your intention might be to "create a successful and innovative business that impacts lives positively."

Combining Action with Positive Energy

The synergy between the Law of Attraction and action is where dreams truly take root and flourish. It's crucial to understand that the Law of Attraction is not a magic wand; it's a co-creative process that requires your active participation. Your thoughts and intentions set the stage, but it's the actions you take that bring your dreams from the ethereal realm into tangible reality.

However, the quality of action matters just as much as the act itself. When action is fueled by positive energy, it becomes a force multiplier. Positive energy, in this context, isn't just a fleeting feeling of happiness; it's a state of alignment with your desires, an unwavering belief that your dreams are attainable. When you combine action with positive energy, you amplify the resonance of your intentions, creating a harmonious frequency that attracts opportunities, resources, and synchronicities.

The secret to harnessing the Law of Attraction lies in cultivating alignment between your thoughts, intentions, emotions, and actions. This alignment is the conduit through which the energies flow seamlessly, propelling you toward the realization of your dreams. Imagine your thoughts as seeds, intentions as the soil, actions as the water, and positive energy as the sunlight. Nurture these elements, and you create the perfect environment for the growth of your dreams.

In the intricate dance of the Law of Attraction, every aspect of your being plays a vital role. Your thoughts, beliefs, emotions, and actions are the brushstrokes on the canvas of your reality. As you paint your dreams with intention and imbue them with positive energy, you create a masterpiece that reflects your deepest desires.

As you navigate this enchanting journey of self-discovery and creation, remember that the Law of Attraction is a dynamic force that responds to your evolving consciousness. Practice mindfulness and self-awareness, for they serve as guides on this transformative path. Embrace gratitude for the manifestations that arise, and continue to refine your intentions as you grow. In this way, you wield the foundation of the Law of Attraction to holding the framework of your life, where dreams take shape and possibilities are boundless.

Maintaining Focus and Consistency

In the exhilarating journey of turning our dreams into reality, there's a stage that often poses a significant challenge—sustaining the momentum. This sub-chapter delves into the vital task of maintaining focus and consistency, which is akin to nurturing a delicate flame to create a roaring fire of achievement. As we navigate this terrain, we'll explore strategies to fend off distractions, design effective routines, and overcome the inevitable lulls that might threaten to stall our progress.

Avoiding Distractions and Shiny Object Syndrome

In our hyper-connected world, distractions seem to be lurking around every corner. The siren call of social media, the allure of new projects, and the constant bombardment of notifications can swiftly lead us astray from our well-charted course. The first step in maintaining focus is awareness. Recognizing the triggers that pull us away from our pursuits is the key to successfully avoiding them.

One powerful strategy is the implementation of intentional boundaries. Designate specific periods of focused work, free from digital interruptions. Turn off notifications, close unnecessary tabs, and create a distraction-free environment. Also, consider the Pomodoro Technique, a time management method that involves alternating between intense work and short breaks. It involves breaking your work into short, focused intervals, usually around 25 minutes, followed by a 5-minute break. This cycle is known as a "Pomodoro." After completing four Pomodoros, take a longer break of around 15-30 minutes. By compartmentalizing your time, you'll be amazed at the surge of productivity that ensues.

Yet, distractions are not solely digital. Internal distractions, such as self-doubt and negative self-talk, can be equally detrimental. Mindfulness practices, like meditation and journaling, help quieten the internal chatter and keep your focus on the task at hand. Visualization can also play a role here—by vividly imagining your dream's realization, you bolster your resolve against distractions.

Developing Routines for Sustained Effort
Routines are the unsung heroes of productivity and consistency. In an often chaotic world, routines provide a reassuring framework that propels us forward, even on days when motivation is scarce. Establishing a routine doesn't mean sacrificing spontaneity; it's about carving out dedicated time for your dreams amid the demands of daily life.

Begin by defining your most productive hours. Are you an early riser or a night owl? Align your routine with your natural energy rhythms. Consistency is key, so commit to your routine, even when enthusiasm wanes. A morning ritual that includes meditation, visualization, and affirmations can set the tone for a focused and inspired day.

Furthermore, leverage the power of habit stacking. Attach your dream-focused activities to existing habits. For instance, pair visualization with your morning coffee or affirmations with your evening skincare routine. This makes your dream work seamlessly integrate into your life.

Overcoming Boredom and Plateaus

Ah, the infamous plateau—a phase that often sows the seeds of doubt and monotony. You've set your sights on the summit, but progress seems to have hit a standstill. In these moments, it's essential to remember that plateaus are not indicative of failure but rather a signpost of growth.

Rekindle your motivation by revisiting your "why." Why did you embark on this journey? What impact will your dream have on your life and the lives of others? Connect with the passion that ignited your pursuit in the first place.

Additionally, embrace a growth mindset. Plateaus are opportunities for learning and refinement. Consider adjusting your strategies, seeking new perspectives, or acquiring additional skills. Remember, a plateau is a temporary pause, not the end of the road.

To combat boredom, infuse variety into your routine. Explore new approaches, incorporate diverse learning methods, and even step out of your comfort zone to explore related areas. Boredom often dissipates when curiosity and exploration take center stage.

Maintaining focus and consistency is the heartbeat of dream realization. By steering clear of distractions, nurturing routines, and surmounting plateaus, you're crafting a path that leads straight to your aspirations. Your journey is a testament to the strength of your commitment and the resilience of your spirit.

Chapter 4: Goal Planning and Strategy

Creating an Effective Goal-Setting Framework

In the grand journey of life, dreams act as our guiding stars. They fuel our passions and inspire us to reach for the impossible. Yet, without a proper roadmap, dreams can often seem elusive, like stars scattered across a vast night sky. This is where the art of goal setting steps in—a transformative process that turns dreams into actionable plans, ensuring that each step taken is a step closer to the destination.

Specific, Measurable, Achievable, Relevant, Time-Bound (SMART) Goals

Imagine standing at the edge of a forest, yearning to reach the other side. Your first instinct may be to rush headlong into the trees, but wisdom lies in planning your path. SMART goals are your compass, guiding you through the wilderness of your aspirations.

Specific: A goal should be as precise as a master craftsman's chisel. Rather than aiming to "get fit," consider a goal like "lose 15 pounds in 3 months through regular exercise and balanced nutrition." Specificity gives your dreams definition and clarity, making them tangible.

Measurable: Progress is like sunshine on a cloudy day—it brightens the journey. Measurable goals, akin to milestones, allow you to track your progress and celebrate the small victories. Numbers, percentages, or deadlines transform vague notions into concrete achievements.

Achievable: Goals are your companions, not unattainable mirages. Dream big, but ground your aspirations in reality. Aiming for a promotion is wonderful, but becoming the CEO by next week might be a stretch. Balance ambition with feasibility for a roadmap that propels you forward.

Relevant: Each goal should connect like the pieces of a puzzle, forming a coherent picture. Goals should align with your overarching dreams and values. If your dream is to become a chef, learning to paint might be a noble endeavor, but mastering the art of culinary delights is your true path.

Time-Bound: Time, like a river, flows steadily forward. Goals are the stepping stones along its banks. Set a deadline for each goal, be it short-term or long-term. This not only instills a sense of urgency but also ensures that your dreams evolve from mere thoughts to manifested reality.

Long-term Goals vs. Short-term Milestones

Just as a skilled architect envisions the entire structure before laying the first brick, a dreamer must embrace both the grand vision and the smaller steps. Long-term goals are the pillars that support your dreams—a career change, writing a book, launching a business. These ambitions demand dedication, persistence, and a clear roadmap.

Short-term milestones, on the other hand, are the bricks that build the foundation. These are the goals that propel you forward on a daily basis—learning a new skill, networking, or completing a course. They're the small victories that accumulate like raindrops, eventually filling the pool of your dreams.

Tracking Progress and Celebrating Achievements
Picture this: you're hiking up a steep mountain. With each step, you're not only getting closer to the summit but also gaining a clearer view of the path you've traveled. Tracking progress works the same way. Regularly reviewing your goals—whether through journaling, spreadsheets, or apps—gives you insights into what's working and what needs adjustment.

And when you hit those milestones, be it climbing the first hill or conquering the mountain's peak, take a moment to celebrate. Acknowledging achievements isn't mere indulgence—it's a powerful way to reinforce positive behavior and motivation. It's like giving yourself a high-five, saying, "Look how far you've come!"

Creating a goal-setting framework isn't just about turning dreams into plans; it's about setting the stage for your personal transformation. Like a sculptor chiseling away the excess to reveal the masterpiece within, setting goals refines your focus, hones your effort, and shapes your journey toward achieving those dreams that once seemed distant stars. Remember, every dream realized is a testament to your ability to set, pursue, and achieve goals that pave the way for an extraordinary life.

Crafting a Personalized Dream Strategy

In the travel of our aspirations, dreams serve as the vibrant threads that weave together the fabric of our lives. Yet, even the most beautiful tapestries require a thoughtful design and careful execution. Just as an artist meticulously selects the hues and patterns, you too can craft a personalized dream strategy that aligns with your unique strengths, resources, and the ever-changing environment.

Tailoring Strategies to Individual Strengths

Imagine a garden flourishing with an array of diverse flowers, each possessing its distinct beauty and qualities. Similarly, our individual strengths are like these flowers – varied and remarkable. Crafting a personalized dream strategy begins with identifying your strengths. These strengths aren't solely confined to talents and skills; they extend to your innate qualities, such as perseverance, adaptability, and empathy.

Consider how your strengths can shape your approach to achieving your dreams. If you're a natural communicator, your strategy might involve networking and building meaningful connections. If you possess analytical prowess, you might focus on data-driven decision-making. By tailoring your strategy to your strengths, you harness your innate capabilities to propel your journey forward.

Leveraging Resources and Networking

In the world of dreams, resources are the tools that help you build your vision from the ground up. These resources encompass not only financial assets but also knowledge, relationships, and experiences. Just as an architect uses various materials to construct a sturdy building, you can leverage your resources strategically to construct the foundation of your dreams.

Networking, a cornerstone of resource utilization, connects you to a vast array of experiences and perspectives. A well-placed conversation might open doors you never knew existed. Moreover, reaching out to mentors or joining supportive communities can provide you with guidance and inspiration.

Consider your network as a garden of potential, where each connection holds the promise of growth. Every interaction, whether a casual chat or a formal meeting, presents an opportunity to learn, collaborate, and expand your reach. By harnessing the power of networking and optimizing your resources, you infuse momentum into your journey toward your dreams.

Adapting Strategies in Dynamic Environments

The world is in a constant state of flux, and so are the paths we tread toward our dreams. An unwavering strategy in a dynamic environment might resemble a sailboat navigating through ever-changing waters – inflexible and prone to capsizing. Instead, adopt the mentality of a skilled sailor who adjusts the sails according to the wind's direction.

Adaptability is the cornerstone of success in shifting environments. Circumstances may alter, new challenges may arise, and unforeseen opportunities may appear. Your strategy should be a living document that evolves alongside your journey. Assess your progress regularly, identify what's working, and refine what isn't.

Flexibility doesn't signify abandoning your dreams; rather, it signifies acknowledging that the path may require detours. This doesn't dilute your commitment; it showcases your resilience and determination to reach your destination, regardless of the route.

In the grand symphony of pursuing dreams, crafting a personalized strategy is the harmonious chord that propels you forward. Tailoring your strategy to your strengths, leveraging resources, and adapting in dynamic environments are the keystones of this harmonious progression. Remember, your dreams are unique, and so too should be the roadmap that guides you.

With each step you take, fueled by your tailored strategy, you inch closer to turning your dreams into reality. So, embrace your strengths, embrace the abundance of resources around you, and embrace the ever-changing journey. Your personalized dream strategy is the compass that will navigate you through the vast landscapes of your aspirations.

Managing Time and Priorities

Time is perhaps the most precious resource we have, and managing it effectively can significantly impact our ability to chase our dreams. In this sub chapter, we'll delve deep into the art of time management and how it intertwines with your dream pursuit. We'll explore techniques to maximize your productivity, strike a balance between your dreams and personal/professional life, and the transformative power of saying no to non-essential activities.

Time Management Techniques for Dream Pursuits

Imagine time as a currency that you must spend wisely. Just as you'd invest money to yield returns, investing your time can bring you closer to your dreams. This technique helps maintain focus, increase efficiency, and prevent burnout.

Another powerful approach is the Eisenhower Matrix. This method categorizes tasks into four quadrants: urgent and important, important but not urgent, urgent but not important, and neither urgent nor important. By categorizing tasks, you can prioritize effectively and allocate your time to tasks that align with your dreams and have the most impact.

Balancing Dreams with Personal and Professional Life

Finding the equilibrium between pursuing your dreams and fulfilling personal and professional responsibilities can be a delicate task. The key lies in setting clear boundaries and managing expectations. Consider creating a schedule that designates specific blocks of time for dream-related tasks, personal activities, and work commitments. This structured approach ensures that you're allocating sufficient time for each aspect of your life, preventing burnout and fostering sustainable progress.

Remember, a balanced life doesn't necessarily mean splitting time equally among all areas. It's about recognizing your priorities and dedicating appropriate time to each, based on their significance in your overall journey.

The Power of Saying No to Non-Essential Activities
Saying no can be empowering, even though it might feel uncomfortable initially. Time is limited, and every commitment you make takes a portion of it. Consider this: Every time you say yes to a non-essential activity, you're saying no to investing that time in your dreams.

Practice the art of selective commitment. Evaluate opportunities, requests, and invitations against your goals. If an activity doesn't align with your dreams, it's perfectly okay to decline gracefully. This doesn't mean shutting yourself off from the world; rather, it's about curating your commitments to serve your bigger purpose.

As you progress on your dream journey, you'll realize that saying no isn't just about protecting your time; it's about valuing your dreams and respecting the effort you're investing to make them a reality.

Managing time and priorities is a skill that can transform your dream pursuit from a distant hope into a tangible reality. By employing time management techniques, balancing your various life aspects, and learning to say no to distractions, you're crafting a life that's intentionally directed toward your dreams. Remember, each tick of the clock is an opportunity, and it's up to you to make the most of it.

Chapter 5: Embracing Failure and Learning

Rethinking Failure as Feedback

Failure is a word that often carries a heavy weight, laden with disappointment, frustration, and a sense of inadequacy. It's a term that we're conditioned to fear, something we're taught to avoid at all costs. Yet, in the intricate dance of pursuing our dreams, failure isn't an adversary – it's an invaluable ally. By reframing failure as feedback, we can unlock a treasure trove of insights that propel us toward greater success and fulfillment.

Extracting Lessons from Setbacks

Every setback, every misstep, and every challenge offers a lesson waiting to be discovered. Think about it: when you encounter an unexpected roadblock on your journey, you're given the chance to pause, reflect, and reevaluate your approach. This isn't a sign of defeat; it's a moment of clarity. Failure often shines a light on aspects that might have been overlooked or underestimated. By dissecting the circumstances surrounding a setback, you can uncover insights that guide your next steps.

The process of extracting lessons from setbacks involves introspection. What were the contributing factors? Were there decisions made in haste? Was there a lack of preparation? By addressing these questions honestly, you can adjust your strategy moving forward. Each failure is a puzzle piece, contributing to the bigger picture of your ultimate success.

Failure as a Stepping Stone to Success

Consider the stories of some of the world's most successful individuals, and you'll find a common thread: they've all faced significant failures along the way. The key difference lies in how they perceived and reacted to those failures. Rather than viewing failure as an endpoint, they saw it as a stepping stone toward their goals.

Failure is a teacher that imparts wisdom through experience. It toughens your resolve, tests your dedication, and encourages you to innovate. In essence, failure acts as a blueprint for growth. When you recognize failure as a natural part of the journey, you free yourself from the fear of it. You're no longer paralyzed by the prospect of failing; instead, you're empowered by the prospect of learning and progressing.

Maintaining Resilience in the Face of Failure

Resilience is the art of bouncing back stronger after adversity. It's the foundation upon which the mindset of successful individuals is built. Maintaining resilience in the face of failure is both an art and a science – it's the ability to recognize the disappointment, process it, and then channel that energy into positive action.

When you encounter failure, it's important to acknowledge your emotions. Allow yourself to feel disappointment, frustration, and even anger. These emotions are valid and human. However, resilience doesn't mean dwelling in negativity; it means acknowledging these feelings and then shifting your focus. Use failure as a catalyst to reevaluate your strategy, refine your approach, and recommit to your goals.

One way to foster resilience is by embracing a growth mindset. Understand that failure is not a reflection of your worth; it's a temporary setback in your journey. As you cultivate resilience, you'll find that failure loses its power to deter you. Instead, it propels you forward, armed with the knowledge that setbacks are the stepping stones that lead to your ultimate triumph.

In the journey of life, failure is merely a note – a note that contributes to the melody of your success. By redefining failure as feedback and approaching it with the intention of learning, you shift your perspective. Setbacks become opportunities for growth, and resilience becomes your guide. The path to your dreams is illuminated not just by your successes, but by the lessons garnered from your failures.

The Growth Mindset and Adaptability

In the pursuit of our dreams, it's inevitable that we encounter obstacles and setbacks along the way. Embracing failure and learning from it is an integral part of the journey toward achieving our goals. This is where the concept of the growth mindset and adaptability comes into play—a mindset that not only welcomes challenges but sees them as opportunities for growth and transformation.

Developing a Resilient Attitude toward Challenges

When we develop a resilient attitude toward challenges, we understand that setbacks are not signs of defeat, but rather stepping stones to success. Instead of being disheartened by failures, we approach them as valuable learning experiences. A resilient mindset allows us to bounce back from setbacks with renewed determination and vigor. It's the understanding that even in the face of adversity, we have the power to shape our responses and navigate difficulties with grace.

Resilience doesn't mean suppressing negative emotions or denying the impact of failure. Rather, it's about acknowledging our emotions, understanding why we feel a certain way, and using these emotions as fuel to drive us forward. Embracing failure with a resilient attitude helps us break free from the fear of failure, allowing us to take calculated risks and venture into uncharted territories with confidence.

Embracing Change and Flexibility

In a world that's constantly evolving, being adaptable is a prized quality. Embracing change and flexibility means being open to new ideas, strategies, and perspectives. It's understanding that as we strive for our dreams, the path may not always be linear. Unexpected changes may force us to adjust our plans, but these detours can lead to new discoveries and opportunities we might have otherwise missed.

Adaptability is not just about surviving change; it's about thriving in dynamic environments. It's about being willing to shed old habits and approaches that no longer serve us, and embracing innovative ways of thinking and doing. This mindset allows us to stay nimble, continuously improve, and stay ahead of the curve.

Transforming Adversity into Opportunities

Perhaps one of the most powerful aspects of the growth mindset and adaptability is the ability to transform adversity into opportunities. When we encounter challenges, setbacks, or even failures, we have a choice: to see them as roadblocks or as openings for growth. Every setback carries with it a hidden gem of knowledge—a lesson that, once learned, can propel us forward.

Think of failure as a teacher—one that provides us with valuable insights about ourselves, our methods, and our goals. Adversity forces us to reevaluate, refine, and sometimes completely reinvent our approaches. It encourages us to question assumptions, experiment with new strategies, and tap into our creativity to overcome obstacles.

By embracing a growth mindset and adaptability, we not only develop the resilience needed to navigate the twists and turns of our journey, but we also cultivate a mindset that's fertile ground for innovation and success. Challenges become opportunities for personal and professional evolution, and setbacks become the catalysts for transformation.

The growth mindset and adaptability form a powerful duo that enables us to view challenges through a different lens—one that sees them not as roadblocks, but as stepping stones to growth. Developing a resilient attitude, embracing change, and transforming adversity into opportunities are key components of this mindset. As we integrate these principles into our journey, we unlock the potential to not only achieve our dreams, but to exceed them, embracing the full spectrum of experiences that life offers us.

Continuous Learning and Improvement

In the journey toward achieving our dreams, we often encounter moments when our best-laid plans don't quite pan out as we envisioned. These moments, though seemingly discouraging, hold within them an invaluable opportunity for growth. In this sub-chapter, we'll delve into the art of continuous learning and improvement—how to cultivate a voracious appetite for knowledge, leverage feedback for personal development, and adapt our dreams based on new insights gained along the way.

Cultivating a Hunger for Knowledge and Growth

Imagine a garden where the seeds of knowledge are sown, tended with care, and nurtured into a lush, thriving landscape. Just as a garden requires consistent attention to flourish, so too does our mind. Cultivating a hunger for knowledge and growth is akin to tending to the garden of our intellect.

Learning doesn't stop when formal education ends; it's a lifelong journey. Nurture your curiosity by exploring topics beyond your comfort zone. Whether it's diving into a new field, reading voraciously, or engaging in thought-provoking conversations, each endeavor contributes to the vibrant culmination of your understanding.

Furthermore, approach challenges as opportunities to expand your skill set. The setbacks and hurdles you encounter provide fertile ground for learning. As you seek solutions, you inevitably acquire new knowledge and insights, bolstering your resilience and equipping you with the tools needed to surmount future obstacles.

Seeking Feedback for Personal Development
Feedback is the compass that guides us toward improvement. It's easy to shy away from criticism, viewing it as a blow to our self-esteem. However, when we shift our perspective, feedback becomes a priceless gift—a chance to refine our skills and better align with our dreams.

Actively seek feedback from mentors, peers, and even those who hold differing viewpoints. Constructive criticism provides a fresh lens through which you can view your progress. Remember, the goal isn't perfection, but progress. By absorbing feedback with an open mind, you'll foster a growth-oriented mindset that propels you forward.

Evolving Dreams Based on New Insights

As we journey through life, our dreams evolve in response to our experiences, new information, and shifting priorities. Embracing change doesn't signify a lack of commitment—it reflects an adaptability that's essential for long-term success.

Regularly assess your dreams in light of your evolving self. Consider the insights you've gained, the lessons you've learned, and the new horizons you've discovered. As your understanding deepens, you might uncover aspects of your dreams that require adjustment. This isn't a setback but a sign of your willingness to stay true to your authentic desires.

Remember that your dreams are dynamic and reflective of your growth. It's natural for them to transform as you gain clarity about what truly resonates with your essence. By embracing the ebb and flow of your dreams, you're not only honoring your journey but also maximizing your potential for fulfillment.

The pursuit of dreams is not a linear path but a symphony of experiences that play a pivotal role in our personal evolution. By cultivating a hunger for knowledge, embracing feedback, and allowing our dreams to evolve, we harness the power of continuous learning and improvement. So, let failures be your stepping stones, feedback your guiding light, and growth your steadfast companion on this remarkable journey of self-discovery and achievement.

Chapter 6: Building Healthy Habits for Success

The Science of Habit Formation

In the symphony of life, habits are the subtle yet powerful notes that compose our daily routines and shape our overall success. The path to achieving our dreams is paved with the small, consistent actions we take each day. In this chapter, we dive into the fascinating realm of habit formation—the science behind why we do what we do, and how we can harness the magic of habits to propel us toward our goals.

Habit Loops and Behavioral Triggers

Imagine your mind as a delicate ecosystem where habits thrive. At the core of habit formation lies the habit loop, a neurological pattern that governs any habitual behavior, from reaching for a cookie when stressed to waking up early to exercise. This loop consists of three parts: the cue, the routine, and the reward.

The cue acts as the trigger that initiates the habit. It could be a time of day, an emotion, a location, or even an event. For instance, feeling stressed (cue) might trigger the habit of mindlessly scrolling through social media (routine), providing a momentary escape and a sense of relief (reward). Understanding these triggers is vital because they offer us the key to unlocking and rewiring our habits.

Habits as Building Blocks of Dream Achievement

Habits, though seemingly inconspicuous, are the cornerstone of our aspirations. They shape our character and determine the direction of our lives. Just as a magnificent building is erected brick by brick, our dreams are realized through the accumulation of intentional habits.

Consider this: The aspiring writer who pens a few paragraphs each morning before dawn, the entrepreneur who consistently networks to expand their business reach, or the musician who dedicates hours daily to mastering their instrument—all are crafting habits that inch them closer to their dreams. By recognizing the profound impact of these daily rituals, we unveil the blueprint for transforming our lives.

Breaking Negative Patterns and Establishing Positive Habits

The canvas of our habits is not always painted with strokes of progress; there are often smudges of counterproductive behaviors. Yet, the beauty of human nature lies in our capacity to change. Breaking free from negative patterns is a testament to our resilience and determination.

To alter a habit, we must not only identify its cues but also substitute the routine with a positive behavior that yields similar rewards. For instance, swapping the late-night snack attack with a calming evening stroll or replacing the time spent on aimless scrolling with reading enriching literature can lead to transformative change.

Establishing positive habits requires more than sheer willpower—it demands understanding the science behind habits and crafting a strategy that aligns with our goals. Start small, with a single habit you wish to nurture. Make it specific, attainable, and attach it to an existing cue. Gradually, layer additional habits onto your foundation, building a harmonious ensemble of actions that lead you toward success.

In the end, our lives are a composition of habits. Every action we take, no matter how seemingly insignificant, contributes to the symphony of our destiny. By mastering the science of habit formation, we equip ourselves with the tools to sculpt our dreams into reality. It's a journey of patience, perseverance, and progress—one habit at a time.

Designing Your Dream Routine

In the symphony of life, routines are the melodies that guide us through each day, creating a rhythm that can lead us toward our aspirations. As you embark on the journey to achieve your dreams, crafting a purposeful routine becomes a compass that keeps you on track, ensuring that each day contributes to your ultimate success. In this section, we delve into the art of designing a dream-centric routine that propels you toward your goals while nurturing your well-being along the way.

Aligning Daily Activities with Dream Goals

Imagine your daily routine as a bridge that connects your present actions to your future accomplishments. The first step in designing your dream routine is to map out how each moment can be in harmony with your goals. Start by identifying the pivotal actions that directly contribute to your dreams. Whether it's practicing a skill, networking, or creating, these actions should take center stage in your daily schedule.

Integration is key. Weave these actions seamlessly into your routine, allowing them to become habitual. This might mean allocating specific time blocks for focused work, practicing discipline to avoid distractions, and aligning your tasks with your peak productivity periods. With time, these deliberate actions will transform into powerful habits that bridge the gap between where you are and where you want to be.

Morning and Evening Rituals for Success

Morning and evening rituals are the bookends of your day – setting the tone for what's to come and helping you unwind. Begin by crafting a morning ritual that energizes and prepares you to seize the day's opportunities. Incorporate activities that resonate with you, such as meditation, journaling, or exercise. These rituals anchor you in a positive mindset, ready to face challenges with clarity and purpose.

Similarly, evening rituals help you wind down and reflect on your progress. This is your time for gratitude, self-assessment, and preparation for the day ahead. Review your accomplishments, acknowledge areas for improvement, and set intentions for tomorrow. These rituals provide closure, ensuring that each day ends on a note of accomplishment and growth.

Nurturing Mental and Physical Well-being
As you journey towards your dreams, remember that self-care is not a detour but an essential part of the path. A well-nurtured mind and body are the engines that drive your aspirations. Incorporate activities that bolster your mental and physical well-being into your routine.

Engage in mindfulness practices that help manage stress, increase focus, and cultivate creativity. Meditation, deep breathing, or even a short walk in nature can do wonders for your mental clarity. Physical exercise is equally vital, not only for your health but also for your productivity. Regular workouts can boost your energy levels, enhance your cognitive abilities, and foster resilience.

Furthermore, don't underestimate the power of rest. Sleep is the cornerstone of well-being. Design your routine to ensure sufficient sleep, for a well-rested mind is more equipped to tackle challenges and explore opportunities.

Your routine is not a set of rigid rules but a flexible framework that aligns with your dreams. It's a dynamic creation that adapts as your goals evolve. Through conscious alignment, purposeful morning and evening rituals, and a commitment to your well-being, your dream-centric routine becomes the vehicle that carries you toward your aspirations. As you integrate these practices into your days, remember that each action, no matter how small, contributes to your journey of success.

Overcoming Procrastination and Distraction

Procrastination and distraction — two common foes that have sabotaged the pursuit of dreams for countless individuals. The battle against these adversaries is one that's fought within the depths of our minds and the environment around us. But fear not, for understanding their origins and employing effective strategies can help us triumph over these challenges and pave the way for a path to success.

Identifying Root Causes of Procrastination

Procrastination is a curious phenomenon. It's that voice in our heads that convinces us there's always a better time to start — tomorrow, next week, or someday in the distant future. But if we peel back the layers, we find that procrastination often stems from a combination of fear, uncertainty, and sometimes a lack of clear goals.

Fear of failure, fear of success, and even fear of the unknown can all contribute to procrastination. These fears create mental barriers that prevent us from taking that crucial first step. The good news is that recognizing these fears is the first step to overcoming them.

Another root cause is often a lack of clarity about the task at hand. When our goals are vague or overwhelming, it's easy to postpone taking action. Breaking down larger tasks into smaller, manageable steps can alleviate this sense of overwhelm and make the process feel less daunting.

Techniques to Overcome Procrastination
Now that we've shone a light on the origins of procrastination, let's delve into techniques that can help you conquer it.

1. The Two-Minute Rule: This rule suggests that if a task can be completed in two minutes or less, do it immediately. This approach prevents small tasks from piling up and creating mental clutter.

2. Pomodoro Technique: This time-management method involves breaking work into intervals, usually 25 minutes of focused work followed by a 5-minute break. After completing four intervals, take a longer break. This structured approach can enhance productivity and help beat procrastination.

3. Visualize the End Result: Imagine the satisfaction of completing the task at hand. Visualizing success can activate your motivation and create a sense of urgency, making it harder to succumb to procrastination.

Creating a Distraction-Free Work Environment
Distractions are the arch-nemeses of productivity. In an era
of constant connectivity, the lure of notifications, social
media, and the ever-scrolling newsfeed can easily derail
our focus. To counteract this, consider crafting a
distraction-free work environment.

1. Designated Workspace: Set up a dedicated area for
work or study. This space should be comfortable, well-lit,
and free from distractions. When you enter this space, your
mind will know it's time to focus.

2. Digital Detox: Temporarily disconnect from digital
distractions. Turn off non-essential notifications, put your
phone on silent mode, and close unnecessary tabs on your
computer. This intentional disconnection creates a bubble
of focus.

3. Time Blocking: Allocate specific time blocks for
focused work. During these blocks, commit to working
solely on the task at hand. Knowing that you have a
designated time for work can motivate you to make the
most of it.

In the journey of success, overcoming procrastination and
distraction is a vital points. By addressing the root causes,
employing effective techniques, and crafting a workspace
that cultivates concentration, you're actively weaving a path
toward achievement. Remember, progress is forged through
consistent effort and a willingness to embrace discomfort.

As you embark on this journey of personal development, keep in mind that conquering procrastination and creating a distraction-free zone are skills that require practice and patience. It's about building a habit of focused work, one stitch at a time, until it becomes an integral part of your success story. So, take a deep breath, visualize the finish line, and let's step boldly into a world of productivity, creativity, and unparalleled accomplishment. Your dreams await your focused attention; it's time to give them the spotlight they deserve.

Chapter 7: Cultivating Positive Relationships

The Influence of Surroundings

In our journey towards achieving our dreams, we often hear the saying, "You are the average of the five people you spend the most time with." It's more than just a catchy phrase; it's a powerful insight into the impact that our surroundings and the people we surround ourselves with can have on our aspirations, mindset, and overall success. In this sub-chapter, we're going to delve into the profound influence of our social circle, the importance of nurturing positive relationships, and the art of setting boundaries to shield ourselves from negative influences.

Recognizing the Impact of Your Social Circle

Take a moment to reflect on the people you interact with regularly – friends, family members, colleagues, mentors, and even acquaintances. Have you ever noticed how their attitudes, beliefs, and energy levels affect your own? Our social circle holds incredible sway over our thoughts and actions, often more than we realize. When we surround ourselves with individuals who radiate positivity, ambition, and support, we naturally absorb these traits. On the other hand, being around constant negativity or discouragement can weigh us down and impede our progress.

In the pursuit of our dreams, it's essential to surround ourselves with individuals who uplift, inspire, and challenge us to become better versions of ourselves. This doesn't mean cutting ties with everyone who isn't in line with our aspirations, but rather being mindful of who we allow to occupy our inner circle. Recognizing the influence of our surroundings empowers us to curate an environment that fosters growth and empowers our dreams.

Nurturing Supportive and Encouraging Relationships
Positive relationships act as fuel for our dreams. They provide the emotional support, motivation, and constructive feedback that propels us forward, even in the face of challenges. Think about the friend who cheers you on when you reach a milestone, the mentor who shares wisdom from their own journey, or the family member who stands by you unconditionally. These connections remind us that we're not alone on our path, and they infuse our journey with a sense of camaraderie.

Cultivating such relationships requires effort and reciprocity. Just as you seek encouragement, be equally invested in supporting others' dreams. Offer a listening ear, provide feedback, and celebrate their achievements. Remember, a network of individuals who genuinely care about your success will always be more valuable than a wide but shallow pool of acquaintances.

Setting Boundaries for Negative Influences
While nurturing positive relationships is crucial, it's equally important to acknowledge the impact of negative influences. Toxic relationships or those that constantly drain your energy can stifle your growth and divert your focus from your dreams. Recognizing when to set

boundaries with such influences is an act of self-care and self-respect.

Setting boundaries doesn't have to be confrontational; it's about preserving your own well-being. Politely decline engagements that don't align with your goals, limit time spent with individuals who consistently bring negativity, and establish guidelines for healthy interactions. Remember, your dreams deserve an environment that allows them to flourish, and that includes protecting your mental and emotional space from harmful influences.

The people we choose to surround ourselves with can either elevate us or hinder us in our quest for success. By recognizing the profound impact of our social circle, nurturing positive relationships, and setting boundaries against negativity, we shape an environment that aligns with our dreams. Remember, you have the power to curate your surroundings, and by doing so, you're taking a significant step towards creating the life you aspire to lead.

Networking for Dream Achievement

In the intricate mosaic of life, our connections with others often serve as the delicate yet powerful threads that interlace the fabric of our journey. It's a dance of shared experiences, ideas, and opportunities that can elevate us to new heights. When it comes to realizing our dreams, these connections become the bridge between aspirations and achievements. Welcome to a realm where networking becomes a potent tool for dream attainment.

Leveraging Networking for Opportunities

Imagine a bustling room alive with conversation, a symphony of mingling, and a vibrant blend of potential connections. Networking, at its core, is more than just a skill; it's an art form that opens doors you might never have known existed. It's easy to think of networking as a purely professional endeavor, confined to suits and business cards. However, the truth is that networking is a blend of artistry and authenticity.

Networking extends beyond the confines of formal events. It thrives in everyday encounters — from your local coffee shop to the virtual realms of social media. It's about being genuinely curious about others, about sharing your story, and, above all, about showing a keen interest in their narratives. By doing so, you plant seeds of connection that can sprout into collaborations, partnerships, and, sometimes, even lifelong friendships.

When we embrace networking as an avenue for dream achievement, we shift the perspective from what we can gain to what we can offer. The act of connecting becomes less transactional and more transformational. The opportunities that flow from these genuine interactions can be astonishing — a mentor who sparks a new vision, a partnership that multiplies your impact, or a resource that propels you toward your dreams.

Effective Communication and Relationship Building
Communication is the brushstroke that paints vibrant hues onto the canvas of relationships. Effective communication goes beyond surface-level exchanges; it's about forging connections through meaningful conversations. It's the art of asking thoughtful questions, listening intently, and responding with genuine interest.

When we communicate with authenticity, we create a safe space for others to share their dreams, challenges, and aspirations. This not only deepens the connection but also lays the foundation for a mutual understanding of how we can support each other. Effective communication is about finding common ground, sharing insights, and, most importantly, being present in the moment.

Building relationships through effective communication is an ongoing process. It involves nurturing connections over time, showing appreciation for others' contributions, and celebrating their successes. Whether it's a quick email to check in or a heartfelt message of congratulations, these small gestures reinforce the fabric of your network.

Offering Value in Interactions
In the field of networking, there's a golden thread that ties everything together: value. When you approach networking with the intention of offering value, you transform ordinary interactions into opportunities for growth and collaboration. Value can come in various forms — from sharing your expertise to making introductions that could open doors for others.

Consider this: by sharing your knowledge and insights, you position yourself as a valuable resource in your network. When you become known as someone who freely imparts wisdom, you create a gravitational pull that draws others toward you. As you offer value, you also set the stage for reciprocity. Others will be more likely to extend a helping hand when they know you're someone who contributes to the collective growth.

Offering value in interactions also means being an active listener. By paying attention to the needs, challenges, and dreams of others, you can identify ways to provide support. It might be as simple as connecting someone with a relevant contact or sharing a resource that addresses a specific concern. These small acts of kindness ripple through your network, strengthening the bonds that tie everyone together.

In the field of networking, the threads you weave are connections that hold immense potential. From opportunities that spark innovation to relationships that foster growth, networking is a cornerstone of dream achievement. So, let curiosity guide you, let authenticity be your compass, and let value be the currency that flows through your interactions. In the end, the mosaic you create will not only enrich your journey but also illuminate the path for others seeking to realize their dreams.

Collaborative Dreaming and Synergy

In the grand mosaic of life, the connections we foster with others are the threads that intertwine dreams and possibilities. Envision a realm where dreams are not solitary pursuits but shared visions that kindle the fires of collective creativity. Welcome to the captivating world of collaborative dreaming and synergy, where the power of unity can propel us to heights beyond imagination.

The Power of Collaboration and Shared Goals

Visualize this: a group of individuals, each bringing a unique set of skills, experiences, and dreams to the table. Now, picture these individuals coming together, sharing their aspirations, and aligning their goals toward a common purpose. This is the heart of collaborative dreaming—a synergy that breathes life into ambitions.

Collaboration is a dynamic force that magnifies what's attainable. By melding diverse perspectives, collaborators infuse their ventures with a richness that stems from varied backgrounds. The true magic emerges when these perspectives coalesce around shared goals. The combined energy of like-minded individuals transforms aspirations into something greater—a vision that transcends individual boundaries and blossoms into a shared dream.

Finding Like-Minded Individuals and Partners

Amidst the journey of life, we often find ourselves drawn to kindred spirits, those who resonate with our visions and values. These like-minded individuals are not just fellow travelers; they are potential collaborators who can elevate our dreams. Identifying them is like discovering hidden gems in the vast landscape of existence.

When you encounter someone who shares your passion and enthusiasm, a seed of collaboration is sown. It's a spark that ignites conversations and inspires the exploration of common ground. This journey of discovery can unfold anywhere—within your social circles, professional networks, or even serendipitous encounters. Each connection has the potential to uncover a fellow dreamer, someone who, when united, can help shape your dreams into reality.

Cultivating a Culture of Mutual Support
Imagine a community where support flows freely, where the success of one is celebrated by all. This is the essence of a culture of mutual support—a fertile ground where dreams are nurtured collectively. In such a community, the growth of each member becomes intertwined with the growth of the whole.

Cultivating this culture requires intention and dedication. It starts with fostering an environment of trust and openness, where individuals feel safe to share their aspirations and challenges. This vulnerability becomes the foundation upon which collaborations are built. As dreams are shared, others can contribute insights, resources, and encouragement—fueling the fire of collective momentum.

In a culture of mutual support, competition gives way to collaboration. Ego takes a back seat to empathy. Each success story becomes an inspiration, reminding us that we are not alone on this journey. When challenges arise, the community becomes a safety net, offering advice, solace, and the wisdom of shared experiences.

In the mosaic of life, collaborative dreaming and synergy are the threads that weave through our existence, binding dreams and hearts together. As you navigate this realm, seek out like-minded souls who share your passions. Nurture connections that are built on shared goals and foster a culture of mutual support. Embrace the power of unity and collaboration, for it is in this harmonious blend that dreams truly come alive, shaping a future that transcends individual horizons.

Chapter 8: Financial and Resource Management

Financial Literacy for Dream Realization

In the grand journey of dream pursuit, your finances play a pivotal role, much like the undercurrents that shape the course of a river. Just as a river navigates its path with a balance of force and finesse, your financial decisions require astute planning and informed choices. Welcome to the realm of financial literacy, where the art of managing your resources paves the way toward the realization of your dreams.

Budgeting and Financial Planning

Imagine your dream as a destination on a map, and your budget as the compass that guides you toward it. Budgeting is not just about tracking your expenses; it's about crafting a roadmap that aligns your financial resources with your aspirations. Think of it as creating a blueprint for your dreams.

Start by examining your current financial landscape. What are your income sources, and what are your regular expenses? Categorize your spending to identify areas where you can allocate more funds toward your dreams. Budgeting doesn't mean sacrificing the joys of today for tomorrow; it's about prioritizing and allocating your resources in a way that supports your dreams without compromising your well-being.

Financial planning extends beyond a mere monthly budget. It involves setting short-term and long-term financial goals that align with your dreams. It's the art of thinking ahead, anticipating potential challenges, and preparing contingencies. By integrating your dreams into your financial plan, you're building a sturdy bridge that connects your aspirations to your fiscal reality.

Investing in Skills and Knowledge
Consider your skills and knowledge as tools that sculpt your dreams into reality. Just as a sculptor refines a piece of art, you can refine your abilities to create the life you envision. Investing in skills and knowledge is a strategic move that can significantly impact your journey toward dream realization.

Identify the skills that are directly aligned with your dreams. These skills could range from technical expertise to soft skills like communication and leadership. Acquiring new skills or honing existing ones not only enhances your competence but also opens doors to new opportunities. Whether it's enrolling in a course, attending workshops, or simply dedicating time to practice, every effort you invest in self-improvement contributes to your dream's foundation.

Knowledge, too, is a currency that appreciates over time. Just as a financial investment yields returns, investing in knowledge yields insights and innovation. Stay curious and curious, reading books, listening to podcasts, and engaging in conversations that broaden your perspective. As you accumulate knowledge, you're equipping yourself with the tools to navigate challenges and seize opportunities.

Balancing Investment Risks and Rewards
Life, like any investment portfolio, comes with a mix of risks and rewards. Just as a wise investor diversifies their assets, you must diversify your approach to risk management. Balancing investment risks and rewards is about making calculated decisions that align with your dreams while safeguarding your financial stability.

When it comes to financial decisions, it's crucial to understand your risk tolerance. Assess your comfort level with different types of risks, whether they're associated with investing, entrepreneurship, or career shifts. A balanced approach involves taking calculated risks that align with your aspirations without jeopardizing your financial well-being.

As you embark on your dream journey, remember that rewards often follow calculated risks. The key is to strike a harmonious balance between chasing ambitious dreams and maintaining a safety net. Explore opportunities, but don't forget to consider potential downsides. Being prepared for both success and setbacks equips you with the resilience to adapt to changing circumstances.

In the journey of your dream realization, financial literacy is the golden thread that binds strategy to action. By mastering budgeting, investing in your skills, and navigating risk, you're not only managing your finances but also sculpting the foundation for your dreams. Consider each financial decision as a brushstroke that contributes to the masterpiece of your life. With mindful planning and informed choices, you're painting a future where your dreams are not just possibilities but tangible realities.

Resourceful Strategies for Limited Resources

In the journey toward achieving our dreams, we often encounter a familiar companion: limited resources. Whether it's time, money, or opportunities, these constraints can feel like barriers to progress. However, in the realm of dream realization, limitations can become the catalysts for innovation, leading us to uncover a treasure trove of resourceful strategies. Welcome to the chapter where scarcity transforms into abundance through ingenuity and determination.

Making the Most of What You Have

Imagine you're handed a handful of seeds and a small patch of soil. Your dream is to cultivate a flourishing garden, but the space and resources are limited. In this scenario, the key isn't in bemoaning what you lack, but in embracing what you possess. Making the most of what you have is the cornerstone of resourceful living.

Just like a skilled gardener maximizes every inch of soil, we too can optimize our available resources. It's about assessing what's at our disposal and leveraging those assets to the fullest extent. This might mean drawing upon your existing skills, networks, or experiences. By recognizing your strengths, you can tap into reservoirs of creativity that lead you to new and unexpected pathways toward your dreams.

Resourcefulness is about understanding that constraints can breed innovation. It's a mindset shift that turns limitations into launchpads. By mastering the art of making the most of what you have, you can transform scarcity into abundance, and modest beginnings into significant accomplishments.

Creative Problem Solving for Resource Challenges
Consider a puzzle: you have a set number of pieces, and the challenge lies in finding ingenious ways to fit them together. Similarly, resource challenges can be approached as intricate puzzles waiting to be solved. Creative problem solving is the tool that enables you to see beyond the obvious and discover innovative solutions.

When faced with a shortage of resources, it's easy to default to frustration or resignation. However, creativity thrives in the face of adversity. It's about looking at a problem from different angles, exploring unconventional avenues, and being open to ideas that defy the norm. By embracing a curious and imaginative mindset, you can uncover hidden gems of possibility.

Think of it as resource alchemy, where limited elements are transformed into valuable assets. Every challenge becomes an opportunity to stretch your problem-solving muscles and hone your adaptability. As you delve into the world of creative problem solving, you'll find that even the most seemingly insurmountable obstacles can be unraveled through innovative thinking.

Identifying Alternative Paths to Dream Fulfillment
Imagine you're driving toward your dream destination, but suddenly, the road you've been following is blocked. In this moment of detour, you have two choices: turn back or explore alternative routes. Similarly, when resources are limited, it's crucial to be open to alternative paths to dream fulfillment.

Resourceful individuals have a knack for finding unconventional avenues to reach their goals. This might involve pivoting from your original plan, embracing unexpected opportunities, or collaborating with unlikely allies. The key lies in remaining flexible and adaptable while maintaining unwavering focus on your dream.

Identifying alternative paths requires a mix of courage and curiosity. It's about being willing to venture into uncharted territory and navigate through uncertainty. By doing so, you're not just creating backup plans; you're opening yourself up to a world of possibilities that you might not have considered otherwise.

In the realm of limited resources, the path to success isn't always linear. It's a dynamic journey that involves embracing change, capitalizing on creative solutions, and pivoting when necessary. By weaving resourceful strategies into the very fabric of your dream pursuit, you'll not only overcome challenges but also uncover avenues of growth and achievement you never knew existed.

As you venture forth with resourceful strategies, remember that limitations are not the end of the road but rather the beginning of a new adventure. Just as a skilled sailor navigates through rough waters, you too can navigate through scarcity to discover the treasures that await on the other side. With every step taken, you're building your own foundation of ingenuity and determination, creating a narrative of success against all odds.

Building Resilience Against Financial Setbacks
Life's journey is an unpredictable voyage, often painted with unexpected twists and turns. Among these, few are as daunting as financial setbacks. In the journey to achieve our dreams, setbacks are the threads of challenge that test our mettle and strength. In this chapter, we'll explore how to stitch resilience into the very fabric of your financial and dream pursuits.

Emergency Funds and Contingency Planning

Imagine this scenario: your dreams are thriving, your plans are flourishing, and then suddenly, an unexpected expense emerges. It's these moments that call for a safety net — a cushion of financial security that prevents a setback from derailing your journey. This safety net is your emergency fund.

The concept is simple: allocate a portion of your income to a dedicated emergency fund. This fund, often forgotten until it's needed, is what grants you the flexibility to weather unexpected financial storms without capsizing your ship of dreams.

Effective contingency planning extends beyond a mere emergency fund. It's about preparing for the unexpected with open eyes. Just as you wouldn't navigate a ship without charts, you shouldn't embark on your dreams without considering potential detours. Assess risks, plan for different scenarios, and craft strategies to navigate through challenging financial waters.

Adaptation in Financially Uncertain Times

Picture this: the market takes an unforeseen dip, economic conditions shift, and suddenly your financial landscape changes. It's in these moments that adaptability becomes your greatest asset. The ability to pivot, recalibrate, and evolve your strategies is what separates the resilient dreamers from the rest.

In times of financial uncertainty, instead of letting setbacks paralyze you, let them inspire you to innovate. Think of these moments as opportunities for growth, where you learn to find value in change itself. It's about adjusting your sails to catch new winds of opportunity, embracing the unknown as a canvas for new beginnings.

Remember, resilience isn't about avoiding setbacks; it's about your response to them. The mindset you cultivate during these times can either stifle your progress or propel you forward. By embracing adaptability, you can navigate even the stormiest financial seas with grace and poise.

Reassessing Goals During Financial Changes
Financial changes are not interruptions but rather threads that add depth and texture to your story of dream. When the financial landscape shifts, it's an invitation to revisit your dreams, realign your goals, and set a new course.

It's essential to differentiate between flexibility and compromise. Flexibility means adjusting the path while staying true to your destination, whereas compromise means sacrificing your dreams due to financial setbacks. Embrace the former; resist the latter.

Reassessing goals doesn't equate to abandoning them. It means recalibrating your expectations, breaking your dreams into smaller, achievable milestones, and gradually rebuilding your momentum. Your dreams remain the North Star; the path you take might just have a few more twists.

Financial setbacks can also foster creative problem-solving. When resources are scarce, ingenuity takes center stage. Your dreams might require you to find innovative, cost-effective solutions, leading to unexpected revelations and growth.

In the journey to achieve your dreams, financial setbacks are but stitches in the narrative. Each setback can teach you to fortify your financial foundation, adapt with resilience, and reorient your course without losing sight of the horizon. Remember, it's not about the setback; it's about the comeback. By embracing the challenge, you thread resilience into the very essence of your journey.

Chapter 9: Impactful Communication Skills

Effective Communication as a Dream Enabler

Communication is the thread that weaves dreams into reality. It's the bridge that spans the gap between the inner world of aspirations and the outer world of achievement. Effective communication isn't just about words; it's about the art of conveying ideas, understanding others, and building bridges of collaboration. Welcome to the realm where communication becomes the catalyst for turning dreams into tangible outcomes.

Articulating Your Dreams and Visions

Imagine standing at the threshold of your dreams, armed with ideas and ambitions that light up your soul. Now, imagine having the ability to convey those dreams to others with such clarity that they can see it as vividly as you do. This is the power of articulation, the art of expressing your dreams and visions in a way that resonates with the hearts and minds of others.

Articulating your dreams isn't just about conveying information; it's about igniting passion and creating a shared vision. Start by painting a picture with your words. Use vivid descriptions that transport your listeners into the world you envision. Whether you're speaking to one person or a group, your ability to articulate your dreams can spark inspiration, rally support, and create a magnetic pull toward your vision.

Remember, it's not just about what you say, but how you say it. Infuse your words with your genuine enthusiasm and belief in your dreams. When you speak with conviction, your words become magnetic, attracting individuals who resonate with your passion and want to be a part of your journey.

Active Listening and Understanding Others
Communication isn't a one-way street; it's a dance of sharing and receiving. Active listening is the secret ingredient that transforms communication from mere exchange to genuine connection. It's about being fully present, suspending your own thoughts, and immersing yourself in the words of others.

When you actively listen, you create a safe space for others to express themselves. You validate their feelings and experiences, fostering a sense of trust and rapport. Through active listening, you gain deeper insights into their perspectives, needs, and aspirations. This, in turn, equips you with valuable information that can help you tailor your message and actions to align with their desires.

Active listening also enables you to uncover hidden opportunities for collaboration. By truly understanding others, you can identify areas where your dreams and visions intersect, creating the potential for mutually beneficial partnerships. Remember, the more you listen, the more you learn, and the stronger your connections become.

Negotiation and Persuasion for Collaboration

In the intricate dance of dream realization, negotiation and persuasion take center stage. These skills aren't about manipulation; they're about presenting your ideas in a way that resonates with others and aligns with their goals. Effective negotiation is the art of finding common ground and reaching agreements that propel everyone forward.

Persuasion, on the other hand, is about influencing others through compelling arguments and genuine passion. It's not about pushing your agenda, but about showing how your dreams and visions can contribute to their success as well. Persuasion is built on empathy and understanding; it's about addressing the needs and concerns of others and demonstrating how collaboration can lead to mutual growth.

Mastering negotiation and persuasion requires empathy, active listening, and adaptability. It's about finding win-win solutions that honor everyone's aspirations. Remember, negotiation isn't about winning a battle; it's about fostering an environment of cooperation and shared progress.

In the field of impactful communication, your words become threads that connect hearts and minds. Articulating your dreams with passion, listening actively to others, and skillfully negotiating and persuading are the tools that shape these threads into bonds of understanding and collaboration. Through effective communication, you don't just share your dreams — you make them come alive in the hearts of others, forging a path toward collective success.

Storytelling for Inspiration and Influence

Imagine a world where words hold the power to shape destinies, inspire action, and forge unbreakable connections. In the intricate field of human communication, storytelling stands as a brilliant framework, holding together experiences, emotions, and aspirations. As we journey deeper into the realm of impactful communication, we uncover the art of storytelling — a transformative tool for inspiration and influence.

Crafting Compelling Personal and Dream Stories

Think back to the tales you heard as a child — stories of heroes, adventures, and magical lands. These narratives captured your imagination and ignited your dreams. Now, it's time to harness that same magic in crafting your own stories.

When it comes to impactful communication, authenticity is your compass. Begin by sharing your own experiences, especially those that resonate with your dreams and aspirations. Paint a vivid picture of your journey, complete with triumphs and challenges. By opening up about your struggles and how you overcame them, you give your audience a relatable entry point into your world.

But don't stop at your personal story. Elevate your narrative by infusing it with your dreams. Describe the vision that propels you forward, the goals you're striving to achieve, and the impact you hope to make. By weaving your dreams into your storytelling, you're inviting others to join you on a compelling journey that holds the promise of growth and transformation.

Sharing Vulnerability and Authenticity

In a world filled with curated images and polished narratives, vulnerability stands as a beacon of authenticity. It's the raw, unfiltered honesty that connects us as humans. When you share your vulnerabilities, you're offering a glimpse into the genuine struggles and doubts you've faced. This vulnerability not only humanizes you but also creates a safe space for others to relate and share their own experiences.

Embrace the power of your imperfections, for they are what make you relatable. Admitting your mistakes, setbacks, and moments of self-doubt invites your audience to see the person behind the story. It also showcases your authenticity, which resonates far more deeply than a facade of perfection ever could.

Remember, vulnerability doesn't equate to weakness. It's a testament to your strength, resilience, and willingness to learn. When you vulnerably share how you've tackled challenges on your path to achieving your dreams, you inspire others to confront their own obstacles with courage and determination.

Eliciting Empathy and Connection through Stories

At the heart of impactful communication lies the ability to foster empathy and connection. And this is precisely where storytelling shines brightest. Stories have the incredible power to evoke emotions, transporting listeners into the shoes of the storyteller. As you share your personal and dream narratives, you're inviting your audience to walk alongside you, to feel what you felt, and to experience your journey as their own.

When crafting your stories, focus on the emotions that underpin your experiences. Describe the excitement of pursuing your dreams, the frustration of facing roadblocks, and the exhilaration of achieving milestones. By allowing your audience to connect with the emotions, you're bridging the gap between your world and theirs.

Eliciting empathy doesn't end with your story. It continues through the lessons you've learned and the insights you've gained. As you reflect on your journey, offer takeaways that resonate universally. Perhaps it's a nugget of wisdom that can help others overcome challenges or a mindset shift that encourages growth. By sharing your lessons, you're imparting value that extends beyond the narrative.

In the field of communication, storytelling is the thread that binds us. It's the conduit through which dreams are passed down, lessons are shared, and connections are formed. By crafting compelling stories, embracing vulnerability, and eliciting empathy, you're not just communicating — you're creating an immersive experience that leaves an indelible mark. So, let your stories be a beacon of inspiration, a mirror of authenticity, and a bridge that unites hearts and minds in a shared journey toward growth and fulfillment.

Overcoming Communication Barriers

In the intricate dance of communication, barriers can emerge like unexpected hurdles, disrupting the flow of understanding and connection. Yet, in a world where effective communication is the cornerstone of success, learning to dismantle these barriers becomes an invaluable skill. Welcome to a realm where communication bridges are built and misunderstandings are transformed into pathways of clarity and connection.

Addressing Misunderstandings and Conflicts

Imagine a conversation as a delicate breeze of words and intentions. Sometimes, however, even gentle wind can make shiver, leading to misunderstandings that cast a shadow over what was meant to be conveyed. Addressing these misunderstandings is akin to unraveling the knots in the thread, restoring the beauty of the conversation.

When misunderstandings arise, it's crucial to approach them with curiosity and empathy. Seek to understand the perspective of the other person, as well as to express your own viewpoint. The key is to communicate openly and respectfully, focusing on finding common ground rather than assigning blame. Often, a simple conversation can untangle the knots and pave the way for a stronger connection.

Conflicts, too, are part of the human experience, and they can arise in both personal and professional interactions. The art of conflict resolution involves active listening, validating feelings, and finding compromise. By approaching conflicts as opportunities for growth and understanding, we can reshape them into catalysts for deeper connection.

Cultural Sensitivity and Inclusive Communication
In the diverse history of humanity, cultural sensitivity is the thread that weaves harmony into our interactions. In an interconnected world, it's essential to recognize and embrace cultural differences, while also avoiding assumptions that can lead to misunderstandings.

Cultural sensitivity begins with a willingness to learn about other cultures and their customs. It's about acknowledging that different backgrounds can shape communication styles, values, and norms. Inclusive communication involves using language that is respectful and inclusive, avoiding any potentially offensive terms or biases.

Embracing cultural sensitivity fosters a sense of belonging and respect among diverse groups. When we make an effort to understand and appreciate each other's perspectives, we create an environment where everyone feels valued and heard. In turn, this paves the way for more meaningful and effective communication.

Effective Virtual Communication in the Digital Age
As technology knits the world closer together, virtual communication has become a cornerstone of modern interaction. However, this new landscape also presents its

own set of challenges, with barriers that can impact understanding and connection.

Virtual communication, through emails, video calls, and instant messaging, demands heightened clarity and intention. Without the nuances of facial expressions and body language, words alone must convey the intended message. This requires careful word choice, tone awareness, and the use of visual aids to enhance understanding.

Furthermore, the digital age calls for digital etiquette. Timely responses, clear subject lines, and concise messages are crucial for effective virtual communication. It's also essential to ensure that technology doesn't replace the human touch; making an effort to schedule face-to-face interactions or video calls can bridge the gap between the digital and the personal.

In a world where screens mediate conversations, the art of listening becomes paramount. Active listening involves not just hearing words, but also understanding emotions and subtext. By embracing active listening in virtual interactions, we show respect for others and create a space where true connection can flourish.

In the realm of communication, barriers can be dismantled, and bridges can be built through conscious efforts. Addressing misunderstandings with empathy, embracing cultural sensitivity, and mastering virtual communication are the keys to effective connection. By weaving these practices into the fabric of our interactions, we can craft conversations that resonate, inspire, and transform.

Chapter 10: Overcoming Fear and Taking Risks

Understanding the Nature of Fear

Imagine standing at the edge of a precipice, gazing down into the unknown. Your heart races, palms sweat, and an uninvited companion known as fear creeps into your thoughts. It's a common human experience — one that we've all encountered on our journey to realizing our dreams. In this chapter, we'll delve into the intricate nature of fear, breaking its door to reveal its dual nature and the profound role it plays in our growth.

Differentiating Between Rational and Irrational Fear

Fear, like a master illusionist, can cloak itself in various disguises. But not all fear is created equal. Understanding the distinction between rational and irrational fear is the compass that guides us through uncharted territory.

Rational fear serves as a protective mechanism, alerting us to genuine threats and dangers. It's the instinct that kicks in when we're faced with an immediate physical risk, such as a car hurtling towards us or a wild animal in our path. Rational fear is built into our DNA, a survival tool honed by eons of evolution.

Irrational fear, on the other hand, emerges from the shadows of our mind, often rooted in the realm of imagination. It's the fear of failure, of judgment, of the unknown. While these fears might lack immediate physical danger, they can be just as paralyzing. These fears often stem from past experiences, traumas, or the whispers of self-doubt that have woven themselves into our psyche.

Embracing Fear as a Catalyst for Growth
Now, here's the twist: fear is not our enemy. In fact, it's a silent companion that can propel us toward personal evolution. Like a gust of wind filling the sails of a ship, fear can give us the momentum to sail beyond our comfort zones and into uncharted waters.

When harnessed, fear becomes a catalyst for growth. It's an indicator that we're pushing our boundaries and venturing into new territory. It's the sensation that accompanies the first step onto a stage, the first word written on a blank page, or the first pitch of a groundbreaking idea. These are moments where fear intertwines with excitement, signaling that we're onto something important.

Embracing fear doesn't mean eliminating it entirely. It means acknowledging its presence, understanding its source, and using its energy to drive us forward. As we walk alongside fear, we redefine it from a paralyzing force to a beacon that illuminates our path toward self-discovery and achievement.

Strategies for Managing and Conquering Fear
The question then arises: how do we navigate this intricate dance with fear? The answer lies in developing strategies that help us manage and conquer our fears, both rational and irrational.

One approach is mindfulness — the art of being fully present in the moment. When we confront fear head-on and observe our thoughts and reactions, we diminish its power over us. We become observers rather than victims, allowing fear to pass through us like a fleeting cloud.

Another technique is reframing. This involves consciously shifting our perspective on fear. Instead of seeing it as a roadblock, we can reframe fear as a sign of growth. By acknowledging that fear is a necessary companion on our journey to success, we can transform it from an obstacle into a stepping stone.

Moreover, cultivating resilience can empower us to face fear with greater strength. Resilience is like a shield that we forge through experience. Every challenge we overcome, every fear we confront, adds another layer to our shield, making us more equipped to weather the storms that lie ahead.

Fear is a thread woven intricately among the fibers of ambition and aspiration. It's a reminder that we're daring to venture beyond the known, into the realm of possibility. As we learn to differentiate between rational and irrational fear, embrace fear as a catalyst for growth, and adopt strategies to manage and conquer it, we unveil a truth: fear, when understood and channeled, becomes a potent ally in the pursuit of our dreams.

Calculated Risk-Taking for Dream Attainment

In the journey to achieve our dreams, the threads of risk
and reward are interwoven in intricate patterns. Risk-
taking, often accompanied by the flutter of uncertainty, can
be a defining moment on the journey to dream fulfillment.
It's a dance between what we stand to lose and what we
stand to gain, and it's a crucial skill that separates the
pioneers from those who remain on the sidelines. Welcome
to the realm of calculated risk-taking—a realm where
dreams are transformed from aspirations into realities.

Weighing Risks Against Potential Rewards

Imagine standing on the edge of a precipice, gazing out at a
vista of possibilities. The chasm before you represents the
risks, while the horizon signifies the rewards. Risk-taking is
not a blind leap into the unknown; it's an evaluation of the
landscape that lies ahead. Every dream, by nature, carries
an element of uncertainty, and it's through skillful risk
assessment that we can make informed decisions.

Weighing risks against potential rewards requires a
discerning eye. It involves considering the best- and worst-
case scenarios and evaluating the potential impact on your
journey. By identifying the potential roadblocks and
detours, you're better equipped to navigate the path to your
dream. Calculated risk-taking isn't about avoiding risk
altogether—it's about understanding the terrain, preparing
for contingencies, and moving forward with a clear-eyed
determination.

Learning from Risks, Successes, and Failures

In the grand journey of life, risks taken are steps that contribute to the rich of experience. Every risk, whether yielding success or leading to failure, holds valuable lessons. Success is a beacon that validates your approach, showing you that your calculations were on point. Failure, on the other hand, provides a treasure trove of insights, revealing the areas that require adjustment.

Learning from risks, successes, and failures isn't just about the outcome; it's about the process. It's about becoming a student of your own journey, extracting wisdom from each step taken. When you view risks as opportunities for growth, you transform fear into a catalyst for personal development. You begin to see that even in the face of failure, you're progressing—because every risk is a stride toward understanding yourself and the world around you.

Building a Resilient Attitude Towards Risks

In the journey of life, a resilient attitude is the thread that unite strength and courage into your core. Resilience doesn't eliminate the fear of risk; it transforms it into a force of empowerment. Building a resilient attitude towards risks involves cultivating the belief that even in the face of uncertainty, you possess the capacity to adapt, learn, and persevere.

Resilience isn't an inherent trait—it's a muscle that strengthens with practice. Begin by reframing failures not as dead ends, but as opportunities to bounce back stronger. Embrace challenges as tests of your tenacity and resourcefulness. This shift in perspective gradually shapes a mindset that views risks as stepping stones, not stumbling blocks.

As you build a resilient attitude, consider fear not as an enemy but as a companion. Acknowledge its presence, but don't allow it to dictate your choices. Instead, let your determination, preparation, and self-belief be the driving factors. A resilient attitude doesn't eliminate the possibility of failure; it ensures that failure is merely a temporary setback, rather than a permanent defeat.

In the journey of dream attainment, calculated risk-taking is the warp and weft that bring depth and texture to your journey. It's the willingness to step beyond the known and embrace the uncertain. By weighing risks against rewards, learning from every experience, and fostering a resilient attitude, you transform risk-taking from a daunting endeavor into an exhilarating leap towards the fulfillment of your dreams. So, stand on the precipice with confidence, gaze at the horizon with anticipation, and take those calculated steps that will ultimately shape the fabric of your success.

Stepping Out of Your Comfort Zone

Imagine standing on the edge of a cliff, looking out at a vast expanse of uncharted territory. It's both exhilarating and terrifying. This moment, right here, encapsulates the essence of stepping out of your comfort zone. It's a dance between the thrill of the unknown and the pull of familiarity. As we delve into this realm, we'll uncover the profound impact that leaving our comfort zone can have on our dreams, growth, and self-discovery.

Expanding Your Horizons for Dream Expansion

Your comfort zone is like a cozy bubble, providing security and familiarity. Yet, within its confines, dreams can remain stifled, and aspirations muted. To achieve greatness, you must first untangle yourself from the tendrils of comfort and embrace the vast expanse beyond.

Dream expansion begins by acknowledging that the unknown holds untapped potential. It's about recognizing that growth occurs when you stretch the boundaries of your experiences. Imagine a world where challenges are invitations and setbacks are lessons. By embracing this mindset, you embark on a journey where each step outside your comfort zone propels you closer to your dreams.

In expanding your horizons, curiosity becomes your compass. Explore new fields, learn new skills, and dare to tread unfamiliar paths. These experiences broaden your perspective, allowing you to see the world through fresh eyes. You unearth hidden talents, discover passions you never knew existed, and develop a deep well of resilience that becomes the foundation of your dream journey.

Gradual Progression in Comfort Zone Challenges

Stepping beyond your comfort zone need not be a leap into the unknown. It's a dance of gradual progression, a rhythm where you challenge yourself in a way that's both empowering and sustainable. Picture a tightrope walker—a master of balance. Each step they take is intentional, calculated, and aligned with their purpose. Similarly, your journey of stepping out of your comfort zone is about crafting deliberate, purposeful challenges that drive your growth.

Start by identifying the edges of your comfort zone—those spaces where you feel a slight unease but also a spark of excitement. These are your launch pads, the springboards from which you propel yourself into new territory. With each small step, you expand your comfort zone's perimeter, transforming it from a circle into a spiral that stretches ever outward.

Celebrating your victories, no matter how small, becomes essential during this journey. Each accomplishment reinforces the notion that you are capable of more than you initially believed. It fuels your confidence, allowing you to tackle bigger challenges with increasing determination. Remember, progress doesn't always mean giant leaps; sometimes, it's about the steady rhythm of those intentional steps.

The Transformative Power of Stretch Goals

Picture a rubber band—it's flexible, adaptable, and capable of stretching beyond its original form. Stretch goals are like that rubber band, except they're not just about reaching further; they're about transforming who you are in the process. These are goals that stretch your capabilities, pushing you to become more resilient, resourceful, and innovative.

Stretch goals challenge the status quo and invite you to step into the shoes of the person you aspire to be. They're not designed to be easily attainable; rather, they demand that you reach beyond your current limitations. In the pursuit of a stretch goal, the focus shifts from the outcome to the journey itself. It's about who you become, the skills you acquire, and the insights you gain along the way.

As you embrace stretch goals, you discover the exhilarating truth: your potential knows no bounds. The fear that once held you back begins to lose its grip, replaced by a sense of purpose that propels you forward. Stretch goals remind you that challenges are opportunities to blossom, and setbacks are merely stepping stones to success.

It's important to note that the pursuit of stretch goals isn't always about the end result; it's about the transformation that occurs along the way. Every step toward a stretch goal is a step away from the familiar and toward the unknown. With each step, you acquire new skills, insights, and perspectives that become part of your personal growth arsenal.

Stepping out of your comfort zone is not a one-time event; it's a mindset and a lifelong practice. It's about embracing uncertainty as an opportunity, seeing discomfort as a stepping stone, and welcoming challenges as catalysts for growth. As you weave your dreams into reality, remember that the threads of courage, resilience, and transformation are woven through the fabric of your journey—one step outside your comfort zone at a time.

Chapter 11: Timeless Principles of Success

The Law of Persistence

In the labyrinth of life's pursuits, where dreams are chased and aspirations soar, there exists an unwavering force that propels the journey forward: persistence. It's the anchor that keeps us grounded in the face of adversity and the engine that drives us toward long-term success. Welcome to a realm where the law of persistence reigns supreme, where the journey is as vital as the destination, and where setbacks are but stepping stones.

Perseverance as the Key to Long-Term Success

Imagine a painter standing before a blank canvas, brush in hand. With each stroke, the masterpiece takes form. Likewise, in the canvas of our dreams, perseverance paints the strokes that create the vibrant illustration of success. Perseverance is more than just sheer determination; it's the unyielding commitment to the path you've chosen, no matter how winding or arduous it becomes.

The journey to success is rarely a straight line; it's a meandering path filled with peaks and valleys. It's during the challenging moments that perseverance shines the brightest. It's the quiet voice within that whispers, "Keep going," when the world seems to whisper, "Give up." Perseverance is the compass that guides us through uncertainty and pushes us to embrace discomfort for the sake of growth.

Perseverance teaches us that the process is just as valuable as the outcome. It's about forging an unbreakable bond with our dreams, nurturing them even when progress seems slow. With each step forward, perseverance reinforces our belief that the journey is worth every ounce of effort we invest.

Bouncing Back from Failures and Setbacks
In the moving forward of life's adventures, failures and setbacks are the threads that add texture and depth to our story. They're not signs of defeat; rather, they're stepping stones toward growth. The law of persistence teaches us that these moments are not dead ends but mere detours on the road to success. It's about bouncing back with renewed vigor and using these experiences as opportunities to learn, adapt, and evolve.

Think of a rubber ball that bounces higher after each impact. Similarly, setbacks are the springboards that propel us to greater heights. They test our resilience, challenge our limits, and refine our strategies. When we adopt the mindset of persistence, failures become temporary setbacks, and setbacks become valuable lessons. It's through this lens that we gain the insight needed to fine-tune our approach and continue our journey with unwavering determination.

Celebrating the Journey of Persistence

In a world fixated on instant gratification, the law of persistence serves as a counterbalance, reminding us that success is a journey, not a destination. It encourages us to savor the process, to relish the challenges, and to celebrate every small victory along the way. The journey is a framework supported with effort, determination, and growth, and each thread adds to the richness of the story we're crafting.

Every step forward, no matter how small, is a testament to our commitment and resilience. Celebrating these milestones fuels our motivation, reminding us of the progress we've made and the hurdles we've overcome. It's about acknowledging the effort poured into each brushstroke, recognizing that success is not an overnight phenomenon but the result of persistent dedication.

As we traverse the landscape of our dreams, let the law of persistence be our guiding star. It's the force that propels us through challenges, the light that illuminates the darkest moments, and the compass that keeps us on course. Embrace the journey, celebrate the victories, and remember that every moment of perseverance is a brushstroke on the canvas of success.

The Principle of Integrity and Ethics

Imagine success not just as a pinnacle to reach but as a journey to navigate, guided by a compass of unwavering principles. In this chapter, we delve into one of the cornerstones of enduring success: integrity and ethics. As we embark on the exploration of this vital principle, we'll uncover how it forms the bedrock upon which true achievement is built.

Upholding Values and Ethics on the Path to Success

Success, when accompanied by integrity, takes on a different hue altogether. It's not just about reaching the destination; it's about the journey that reflects who you are as a person. Upholding your values and ethics is not a mere option; it's a conscious choice that you make at every crossroad.

Integrity is your compass in the tumultuous seas of decision-making. It's about adhering to your core values even when the tide of convenience and temptation pushes against you. When your actions are in alignment with your values, success becomes not just an external marker but an internal affirmation of your character.

Ethics, too, are the guideposts that help you navigate the often-murky waters of achievement. It's about asking yourself the tough questions: Are my actions honest? Am I treating others with respect and fairness? When you operate within ethical boundaries, you create a ripple effect that extends beyond your immediate success. You set an example that inspires others to follow suit.

Trust-Building Through Authenticity and Transparency
In the interconnected world we live in, trust is the currency that fuels relationships, collaborations, and opportunities. Trust is built not through glossy facades but through authenticity and transparency. It's about showing up as your true self, flaws and all, and letting your actions speak louder than your words.

Authenticity is a magnet that draws people toward you. When you're genuine and unafraid to show your vulnerabilities, you create a space where others feel safe to do the same. Authenticity fosters genuine connections that have the potential to become a network of support and collaboration.

Transparency is the window through which others see into your intentions and actions. It's about being open and honest in your dealings, even when the truth might be uncomfortable. When you communicate openly about your successes and challenges, you not only build trust but also demonstrate that your journey is grounded in reality, not myth.

Together, authenticity and transparency lay the foundation for relationships that endure. People are drawn to those who are honest about their journey, who don't shy away from admitting mistakes, and who celebrate successes with humility. When you show up authentically and transparently, you're not just succeeding; you're inspiring and empowering those around you.

Navigating Ethical Dilemmas with Integrity
The path to success is rarely without its ethical challenges.
It's in these moments of ethical dilemma that your character
shines the brightest. Navigating these waters requires a
steady moral compass, and that compass is integrity.

Integrity compels you to choose the right course of action,
even when it's the harder path. It's about asking yourself:
What action would align with my values? What choice
would I be proud to defend? In these moments, success
takes a back seat to doing what's right.

When faced with ethical crossroads, take a step back and
consider the consequences of your choices. Think about the
impact your decisions might have on others, your
reputation, and your own sense of self. It's through these
ethical dilemmas that you carve out the essence of your
success story.

In a world that's often focused on instant gratification,
enduring success is rooted in timeless principles.
Upholding values, practicing ethics, and navigating with
integrity are the cornerstones that not only elevate your
achievements but also create a legacy that stands the test of
time. As you weave the fabric of your journey, let integrity
and ethics be the golden threads that shine through, making
your success not just remarkable, but truly meaningful.

The Importance of Giving Back

In our journey to success, there lies a thread that, when woven with intention and heart, adds a richness and depth beyond measure. This thread is the act of giving back, a principle that transcends time and resonates through the ages. It's a profound recognition that the journey to success isn't just a solo expedition; it's a shared adventure that becomes more meaningful when we uplift others along the way.

The Reciprocal Nature of Generosity

Generosity is a force that defies logic. It seems that the more we give, the more we receive in return. But let's not mistake this for a mere transaction. The reciprocity of generosity is not about expecting something in exchange; it's about the energy we create in the act of giving.

When we give from a place of genuine care and compassion, we create a ripple effect that touches lives far beyond our own. Think about the times when someone's kindness illuminated your path or when a mentor's guidance changed the course of your journey. Each of these instances represents the cycle of generosity in action.

The beauty of this reciprocity lies in its authenticity. It's not about giving to get; it's about giving to ignite positive change. When we selflessly contribute to the well-being of others, we create an environment where kindness and support flourish. This environment becomes the fertile ground in which dreams take root and bloom.

Impactful Ways to Contribute to Others
Giving back isn't confined to grand gestures; it's a practice that can be woven seamlessly into our daily lives. The impact of our contributions doesn't hinge on the magnitude of the act, but rather on the intention behind it. Here are some impactful ways to contribute to others:

1. Sharing Knowledge: One of the most powerful gifts you can offer is your knowledge and expertise. Whether through mentorship, workshops, or online resources, sharing what you've learned can guide others toward their aspirations.

2. Acts of Kindness: Small acts of kindness have a profound effect. A smile, a genuine compliment, or a helping hand can brighten someone's day and create a ripple of positivity.

3. Supporting Dreams: Taking the time to listen to someone's aspirations and offering encouragement can be transformative. Your belief in their potential can ignite a newfound sense of determination.

4. Volunteering: Contributing your time and energy to a cause you care about not only benefits others but also enriches your own sense of purpose and fulfillment.

5. Creating Opportunities: Whether it's connecting someone to a valuable contact or recommending them for an opportunity, your actions can open doors that lead to success.

6. Empathy and Compassion: Sometimes, the most impactful contribution is simply being there for someone, offering a listening ear, and showing empathy during their challenges.

Fostering a Legacy of Positive Influence

As we journey toward success, we're not just building a path for ourselves; we're shaping a legacy that extends beyond our lifetimes. Giving back becomes the legacy we leave behind — a legacy of positive influence and transformative change.

When we embrace the importance of giving back, we become part of a collective effort to uplift humanity. We join a lineage of individuals who understood that success isn't merely about personal gain; it's about the imprint we leave on the world. It's about contributing to a larger narrative of progress and betterment.

Imagine the impact if each person on their path to success paused to offer a helping hand to someone else. The ripples of these actions would intertwine, forming a beautiful painting of interconnected dreams and achievements. Each act of giving back becomes a painting in this grand museum, telling a story of shared aspirations and collective growth.

The principle of giving back is a testament to the interconnectedness of our journeys. It's a reminder that success is not a solitary pursuit; it's a collaborative endeavor. So, let your journey be defined not only by your personal achievements but also by the positive influence you exert on others. As you contribute to the dreams of others, you'll find that your own journey is elevated in ways you never could have imagined.

Chapter 12: Embracing Gratitude and Mindfulness

Practicing Gratitude for Dream Fulfillment

In the hustle and bustle of chasing our dreams, it's easy to get caught up in the whirlwind of aspirations and achievements. But have you ever paused to consider the remarkable power of gratitude on this journey? Gratitude isn't just a fleeting emotion; it's a transformative practice that can infuse your pursuit of dreams with a sense of purpose, fulfillment, and abundance. In this subchapter, we'll explore how practicing gratitude can be the compass that guides you to the realization of your dreams.

Recognizing and Appreciating Progress Made

Imagine standing at the base of a towering mountain, eyes fixated on the distant peak. While the summit may be your ultimate goal, remember that every step you take along the path is an accomplishment in itself. Practicing gratitude means taking a moment to turn around and admire the trail you've blazed so far.

When you pause to recognize and appreciate the progress you've made, you're acknowledging the effort, dedication, and courage that have brought you to where you are today. This simple act of reflection not only fuels your motivation but also nurtures a sense of accomplishment that propels you forward. Gratitude redirects your focus from what's still on the horizon to the milestones that mark your journey.

The Connection Between Gratitude and Abundance
Gratitude has a way of shifting our perspective from scarcity to abundance, from what's lacking to what's present. The act of being thankful for what you have is like a magic spell that opens your eyes to the richness that surrounds you. When you immerse yourself in gratitude, you're aligning your energy with the universe's endless possibilities.

Consider how this aligns with your dreams. By cultivating a mindset of abundance, you're setting the stage for your dreams to flourish. You're inviting the universe to conspire in your favor, drawing in opportunities and resources that resonate with your aspirations. Gratitude becomes the fertile ground where your dreams can take root and bloom.

Daily Rituals of Gratitude for Mental Well-being
Just as a garden needs regular tending to thrive, your mindset requires consistent care. Introducing daily rituals of gratitude into your life can be a transformative practice that nurtures your mental well-being. Imagine starting each day with a moment of reflection, where you consciously express gratitude for the gifts in your life.

This ritual can be as simple as jotting down three things you're grateful for each morning. It might be the warmth of the sun on your skin, the support of loved ones, or the progress you've made on your journey. As you anchor your mind in gratitude, you're setting a positive tone for the rest of the day. This practice also serves as a gentle reminder that even amidst challenges, there's always something to be thankful for.

Beyond mornings, you can infuse gratitude into your daily routine. Whether it's a moment of reflection before bed or a pause during a busy day, these pockets of gratitude become touchstones that anchor you in the present moment. They provide a respite from the whirlwind of dreams and obligations, offering a sanctuary of calm and appreciation.

In the symphony of your dream pursuit, practicing gratitude becomes the soothing melody that harmonizes your efforts. It grounds you in the present, reminds you of the progress you've made, and draws your attention to the abundance that's woven into every thread of your journey. So, as you navigate the labyrinth of aspirations, don't forget to pause and express gratitude. For it's in these moments of appreciation that the magic of your dreams truly comes alive.

Cultivating Mindfulness for Dream Focus

In the hectic day of our modern lives, it's easy to get swept up in the current of constant activity. The never-ending to-do lists, the barrage of notifications, and the relentless pursuit of goals can leave us feeling like we're on a runaway train, hurtling forward without a moment to catch our breath. That's where mindfulness steps in — a gentle guide that helps us navigate the chaos with clarity and purpose, ultimately enhancing our ability to focus on our dreams and aspirations.

Mindfulness Techniques for Concentration

Imagine sitting at your desk, fully immersed in the task at hand. Your mind isn't racing with worries about the future or regrets about the past. Instead, it's anchored firmly in the present moment, attentive to every detail and nuance. This state of focused awareness is the essence of mindfulness, and it holds immense power when it comes to dream pursuit.

Mindfulness techniques can work wonders for enhancing concentration. One such technique is mindfulness meditation. It's a practice that involves sitting in a comfortable position, focusing on your breath, and gently redirecting your attention whenever your mind starts to wander. Over time, this exercise trains your mind to stay present, allowing you to approach your dreams and tasks with heightened concentration.

Another technique is the "one-tasking" approach. In a world that glorifies multitasking, this technique encourages you to give your full attention to a single task at a time. By immersing yourself in the present task without distractions, you not only boost your productivity but also engage more deeply with the process. This focused attention is a cornerstone of dream achievement.

Managing Stress and Overwhelm through Mindfulness
Dream pursuit can sometimes feel like juggling a multitude of responsibilities, leaving you feeling overwhelmed and stressed. This is where mindfulness comes to the rescue, offering a calming balm for the stormy seas of stress. By practicing mindfulness, you learn to observe your thoughts and emotions without judgment, creating a buffer between you and the chaos.

When stress arises, mindfulness encourages you to take a step back and become an observer of your thoughts. This simple act can prevent you from spiraling into a cycle of negativity. It's like taking a pause before reacting, allowing you to respond with clarity and composure.

Mindfulness techniques, such as deep breathing exercises or body scans, can be invaluable tools for managing stress in the moment. They anchor you in the present, drawing your focus away from worries about the future or regrets about the past. As a result, you're better equipped to handle challenges with a calm and collected mindset.

Balancing Reflection with Forward Momentum
Dream pursuit is a dynamic journey that requires a delicate balance between reflection and action. Mindfulness offers a bridge between these two aspects, allowing you to reflect on your progress while maintaining the momentum needed to move forward.

Mindful reflection involves setting aside time to review your journey, acknowledging your achievements, and

identifying areas for growth. This practice is like taking a
compass reading — it helps you course-correct and stay
aligned with your dreams. It's a chance to celebrate how far
you've come and recalibrate your path if needed.

However, mindful reflection is not about dwelling in the
past. It's about gleaning insights that propel you forward.
By maintaining a mindful awareness of your thoughts and
emotions, you can identify any self-limiting beliefs or
patterns that might be hindering your progress. This self-
awareness is the foundation upon which you can build a
future filled with purpose and intention.

As you navigate the intricacies of dream achievement,
remember that mindfulness is your steadfast companion.
It's the lantern that illuminates your path, helping you to
focus on the present moment, manage stress with grace,
and strike a harmonious balance between looking back and
moving forward. By embracing mindfulness, you enrich
not only your journey but also your inner landscape,
cultivating the fertile ground from which dreams can
flourish.

Savoring Success and Joyful Moments

Amidst the whirlwind of chasing dreams and scaling heights, it's all too easy to overlook the small yet profound moments of victory that pepper our journey. In a world perpetually focused on the next achievement, taking a pause to savor the sweet taste of success becomes an art worth mastering. So, let's delve into the practice of not just achieving milestones, but also relishing them with an open heart.

Celebrating Milestones and Achievements

Imagine standing on a mountaintop, gazing down at the trail you've traversed to reach this point. Every step, every challenge conquered, and every aspiration pursued culminate in the panoramic view before you. This is the essence of celebrating milestones — acknowledging the distance you've covered and the progress you've made.

Milestones come in all shapes and sizes, from the grand triumphs that make headlines to the quiet victories that only you truly understand. Whether it's landing that long-awaited contract, completing a course you embarked upon, or even mastering a new skill, each achievement is a testament to your dedication and resilience.

Celebrating milestones isn't just about the destination; it's about recognizing the journey that led you here. Pause, take a breath, and let the gravity of what you've accomplished sink in. Allow yourself a moment of pride, for these milestones are the building blocks that pave the way for greater achievements.

The Emotional Impact of Acknowledging Success

Have you ever noticed the warmth that spreads through your chest when you acknowledge a personal success? That's the emotional impact of giving yourself permission to bask in your accomplishments. It's not just about the external recognition you receive; it's about the internal validation that lights a spark within you.

When you acknowledge success, you send a powerful message to your subconscious mind — a message that says, "I am capable, and I am deserving." This affirmation has a profound impact on your self-esteem and confidence. It fuels a positive cycle: as you recognize your successes, you cultivate a sense of self-worth that propels you toward even greater triumphs.

Moreover, acknowledging success amplifies your emotional connection to your dreams. It reinforces the belief that your aspirations are not distant stars but achievable realities. As you feel the emotions that accompany success, you infuse your dreams with life, making them tangible and real.

Incorporating Joy as Fuel for Dream Pursuits

Imagine a sailboat propelled by the wind — joy is that wind for your dreams. When you incorporate joy into your journey, you transform the pursuit of dreams from a grueling task into a delightful adventure. Joy is the driving force that keeps you moving forward, even in the face of challenges.

Consider this: when you savor the joy of every small success, you infuse your journey with positivity. Each moment of joy becomes a stepping stone that propels you toward your next goal. Joy doesn't just coexist with success; it amplifies it, making your achievements even more meaningful and fulfilling.

Incorporating joy into your dream pursuits is about finding delight in the process, not just the outcome. It's about infusing creativity, playfulness, and enthusiasm into your everyday actions. When you infuse joy into your work, you transform it from a chore into a passion.

Each milestone achieved is a testament to your dedication, each success acknowledged is a boost to your self-worth, and each moment of joy embraced is fuel for your future pursuits. So, celebrate your milestones, acknowledge your successes, and infuse your journey with joy. As you savor each victory, you create a symphony of fulfillment that reverberates through every aspect of your life.

Chapter 13: Reshaping Perceptions of Success

Redefining Success on Your Terms

In the ever-evolving narrative of human existence, the concept of success has often been painted with a broad brush, molded by society's expectations, media portrayals, and the whispers of well-meaning acquaintances. Yet, the canvas of success is one that each of us holds a brush to — and it's time we painted a picture that resonates with our own hues. Welcome to the realm where you wield the power to redefine success on your terms.

The Danger of External Definitions of Success

Picture this: A protagonist's journey in a novel dictated solely by the script of others. The plot twists are predictable, the climax lacks intensity, and the resolution feels unsatisfying. In much the same way, adhering solely to society's definitions of success can leave us with a life that feels borrowed, a dream unfulfilled. It's a cautionary tale of chasing goals that are not aligned with our true desires.

Society often presents a predefined path to success — the corner office, the luxurious lifestyle, the praise of others. Yet, this path is often fraught with pitfalls, as it overlooks the inner landscape of the individual. The danger lies in surrendering our own aspirations to external benchmarks. It's akin to wearing a mask that conceals our authentic selves.

The liberation comes when we embrace the audacious notion that success isn't a one-size-fits-all costume. It's a bespoke suit that should reflect our uniqueness, our passions, and our values. Recognizing the danger of external definitions of success is the first step toward reclaiming your narrative, a narrative rooted in authenticity and self-discovery.

Personalizing Success for Fulfillment

Think about success as an exquisitely tailored outfit. It should be comfortable, fitting you like a second skin, and enhancing your confidence as you stride through life. To personalize success is to weave your essence into the fabric of your journey. It's about discovering what truly ignites your spirit and aligning your pursuits with those inner flames.

Personalizing success requires introspection, a deep dive into your desires and dreams. It's about distilling the essence of what brings you joy, what fuels your curiosity, and what resonates with your heart's whispers. This process might involve shedding notions of success that were never yours to begin with — the job title you never truly desired, the accolades that felt hollow.

As you unearth the elements that define your unique version of success, you pave the way for fulfillment. This isn't merely success that's visible on the surface; it's a success that seeps into the core of your being. It's a success that energizes you when you wake up and gives you a sense of purpose as you lay your head to rest. Personalizing success is about creating a narrative that resonates within you, a story that's authentically yours.

Measuring Success Beyond Material Achievements
Imagine a life where success isn't measured solely by bank balances and possessions. Instead, success is a stronghold with support of experiences, relationships, and personal growth. It's about moving beyond the material markers and embracing the intangible aspects that contribute to a meaningful existence.

In a world driven by metrics and benchmarks, it's easy to overlook the immeasurable moments that make life rich. Success isn't just about the numbers on a paycheck or the square footage of your house; it's about the quality of your connections, the depth of your passions, and the fulfillment you find in pursuing your dreams.

By measuring success beyond the material realm, you free yourself from the confines of comparison and the relentless pursuit of more. You grant yourself permission to celebrate the small victories — a heartwarming conversation, a personal breakthrough, a moment of profound clarity.

In the journey of life, success isn't a fixed destination but a dynamic voyage. It's a path that winds through the terrain of your aspirations, your growth, and your true self. Redefining success on your terms means acknowledging the danger of external definitions, infusing your journey with personal fulfillment, and recognizing that the measure of success is far grander than material possessions. As you wield the brush to paint your own canvas of success, remember that the masterpiece you create is uniquely yours, a reflection of the extraordinary journey you've embarked upon.

The Pursuit of Happiness Alongside Dreams

In the grand adventure of life, there's a common thread that binds us all: the pursuit of happiness. It's an age-old quest, woven into the very fabric of our existence. And yet, in our pursuit of dreams and ambitions, we often find ourselves at a crossroads where the pursuit of happiness seems to diverge from the path of achievement. But here's the secret that the journey of a dreamer unveils: happiness and dreams aren't divergent trails; they're interconnected roads that can lead us to a more fulfilled and joyful life.

Integrating Joy and Satisfaction into the Journey

Picture this: You're amidst a bustling crowd, achieving milestones, and chasing aspirations. It's easy to get swept up in the whirlwind of to-do lists and ambitions. But amidst this frenzy, we often forget that the journey itself holds immense value. It's not just about reaching the destination; it's about savoring every step along the way.

Integrating joy and satisfaction into the journey doesn't mean diluting your ambitions; rather, it's about infusing each moment with purpose and appreciation. It's the art of celebrating not only the big wins but also the small victories, like the insights gained from failures and the progress made through persistent effort.

Imagine the satisfaction that comes from setting aside time to reflect on how far you've come. This practice not only enhances your self-awareness but also provides a reservoir of motivation. It's the realization that the pursuit of dreams is a sketch of experiences, each contributing to the masterpiece of your life.

Balancing Ambition with Emotional Well-being
As dreamers, ambition courses through our veins like a driving force. But while ambition propels us forward, it's essential to recognize when it threatens to overshadow our emotional well-being. Balancing ambition with emotional well-being is the art of recognizing when to press forward and when to pause and recharge.

The pursuit of happiness alongside dreams requires a delicate equilibrium. It's about recognizing the signs of burnout and stress and taking proactive steps to address them. This might mean setting boundaries to protect your precious time, prioritizing self-care rituals that nurture your spirit, or seeking solace in activities that bring you genuine joy.

Consider this: In the grand symphony of your journey, emotional well-being is the rhythm that keeps everything harmonious. When you're attuned to your own emotional needs, you're better equipped to navigate challenges with resilience and approach victories with a balanced perspective.

Finding Happiness in Progress and Growth
One of life's greatest ironies is that while we're so focused on the end result, it's often the process of progress that brings us the most happiness. Every step toward your dream is a testament to your growth, a brushstroke on the canvas of your journey. It's these brushstrokes that create a masterpiece worth celebrating.

Finding happiness in progress doesn't mean settling for mediocrity; rather, it's about shifting your focus from what's ahead to what's happening now. It's about finding joy in the daily disciplines that inch you closer to your dream. It's the joy of learning, of overcoming obstacles, and of becoming the person you need to be in order to grasp your dreams.

Imagine the feeling of accomplishment that comes from looking back and realizing the hurdles you've conquered and the fears you've faced. This realization becomes a source of enduring happiness, a reminder that every effort counts, and every step brings you closer to the summit of your dreams.

In the grand journey of life, the pursuit of happiness is not a detour from your dreams; it's an integral part of the route. It's about recognizing that the joy you experience along the way is just as significant as the destination you're striving for. So, let the pursuit of happiness be your compass, guiding you through the highs and lows of your journey. Embrace every step, celebrate every milestone, and remember that happiness is not just a destination—it's a companion on the grand adventure of realizing your dreams.

Achieving Balance in a Hyper-Connected World

In a world that's always "on," where notifications dance across our screens and the pressure to hustle never seems to fade, achieving balance might feel like chasing a mythical creature. Yet, the pursuit of our dreams doesn't have to come at the cost of our well-being. Let's unravel the art of finding equilibrium in a hyper-connected world, where dreams can flourish without sacrificing our mental, emotional, and physical health.

Escaping the Trap of Constant Hustle

The modern era glorifies the hustle — the relentless pursuit of goals, often at the expense of rest and rejuvenation. We've been conditioned to believe that success requires burning the candle at both ends, but this mindset comes at a steep price. The constant hustle can lead to burnout, strained relationships, and a sense of emptiness despite material achievements.

Escaping this trap begins with a shift in mindset. Instead of valuing busyness as a badge of honor, we must recognize that our best work emerges when we're rested and mentally clear. It's about choosing purposeful productivity over mindless multitasking. When we embrace the idea that success doesn't hinge solely on the number of hours worked, we liberate ourselves from the cycle of perpetual busyness.

Strategies for Setting Boundaries and Prioritizing Self-care

Boundaries are the fortresses we build to protect our dreams, aspirations, and well-being. Setting boundaries doesn't mean turning away from opportunities; it's about safeguarding your energy and time for what truly matters. This might involve designating specific work hours, unplugging from digital distractions during personal time, or learning to say "no" when commitments infringe upon your balance.

Prioritizing self-care isn't selfish; it's an act of self-preservation. Just as an athlete can't perform well without adequate rest, you can't pursue your dreams effectively without nurturing your body and mind. Incorporating regular exercise, meditation, hobbies, and time with loved ones isn't a luxury — it's essential. When you're balanced and whole, your creativity flourishes, and your ability to navigate challenges strengthens.

Creating a Holistic Approach to Dream Pursuits
Dreams don't flourish in isolation; they thrive when woven into the fabric of a well-rounded life. The pursuit of success should be harmonious with your overall well-being, relationships, and passions. Creating a holistic approach to dream pursuits means recognizing that your aspirations are just one part of a rich and interconnected line of experiences.

Integrating your dreams into your life involves aligning your goals with your values. It's about understanding that sacrificing happiness for achievement isn't a sustainable path. When you approach your dreams with a holistic mindset, you begin to see opportunities for growth in every aspect of your life. Your relationships, health, and personal development become interconnected sources of strength that nourish your dreams.

Finding this balance might require periodic reassessment. As your dreams evolve, so should your approach to achieving them. Just as a tree needs strong roots to grow tall, your dreams need a foundation of well-being and balance to flourish. So, take moments to reflect, adjust, and ensure that your dream pursuit remains aligned with your authentic self.

In a hyper-connected world, the key to dream achievement isn't to dive headfirst into the chaos; it's to dance gracefully amid it. By escaping the hustle trap, setting boundaries, and embracing a holistic approach, you build a sustainable path to success—one that's marked not only by accomplishments but by the harmonious symphony of a well-lived life. Remember, your dreams are a part of your life, not the entirety of it. In finding balance, you're not just achieving your dreams; you're achieving a fulfilled and vibrant existence.

Chapter 14: Navigating Setbacks and Plateaus

Dealing with Dream Plateaus

Life's journey resembles a symphony, with ebbs and flows, crescendos, and, yes, moments of stillness. Just as a river finds its resting pools amidst its rush, our pursuit of dreams often encounters plateaus—those stretches where progress seems to stand still. While plateaus can be frustrating, they are an integral part of the journey, offering profound lessons and opportunities for growth. In this subchapter, we'll explore the art of navigating dream plateaus, reigniting the fire within, and persevering through the challenges.

Recognizing and Accepting Plateau Phases

Imagine hiking up a mountain: after an arduous climb, you find yourself on a vast, level plateau. Similarly, the path to your dreams can sometimes level out, leaving you wondering if you've hit a wall. Plateaus can manifest as periods of stagnant growth or seemingly insurmountable challenges. But take heart—these moments are not signs of failure; they're reminders of the need for adjustment.

Recognizing a plateau is the first step to understanding its role in your journey. Instead of resisting it or allowing frustration to take root, embrace this phase as a vital component of growth. Plateaus often arrive as invitations to reflect, reassess, and recalibrate your course. It's a natural time to evaluate your strategies, celebrate your progress so far, and realign your focus.

Strategies to Reignite Passion and Motivation

So, you've found yourself on a plateau. Now what? It's time to tap into your wellspring of creativity and determination. One of the keys to navigating a plateau is to reignite the passion that sparked your dreams in the first place. Reflect on what ignited your enthusiasm and explore new angles or approaches to your pursuits.

One strategy is to break down your larger dream into smaller, achievable milestones. These mini-goals not only provide a sense of accomplishment but also keep the fire of motivation burning. Additionally, injecting novelty into your routine can infuse excitement. Consider learning a new skill, exploring a related interest, or seeking fresh perspectives through books, workshops, or engaging conversations.

Staying Committed During Challenging Times

Plateaus aren't the only challenges life throws our way. External factors, unforeseen obstacles, and even self-doubt can join forces, creating a stormy sea of challenges. During these times, your commitment to your dreams is tested. Staying steadfast requires an unwavering belief in your potential, even in the face of adversity.

Remind yourself of the progress you've made. Often, we're so focused on the distance we have yet to cover that we overlook the ground we've gained. Reflecting on your journey so far can reignite the spark of determination. Surround yourself with a support system—friends, family, mentors, or even a community of like-minded dreamers—who can provide encouragement, wisdom, and perspective.

In challenging times, self-compassion is paramount. Acknowledge that setbacks are a universal part of the journey, not an indication of inadequacy. Allow yourself space to regroup, recalibrate, and recharge. As you weather the storms, remember that the choice to keep moving forward, even in the face of difficulties, is a testament to your resilience and dedication.

Dealing with dream plateaus isn't an exercise in frustration but an opportunity for transformation. By recognizing these phases, reigniting your passion, and staying committed, you create a roadmap to navigate these moments with grace and insight. Just as a river's pace may vary on its course, the journey toward your dreams can include moments of steady progress, sharp turns, and, yes, plateaus. Embrace them as valuable chapters in the story of your growth and achievement.

Strategies for Bouncing Back from Life Setbacks

Life's journey is never a straight path; it's an intricate maze of twists, turns, and unexpected obstacles. Setbacks are the ripples in the pond, the detours that challenge our resolve and test our mettle. But it's precisely in these moments of difficulty that our true strength emerges. In this chapter, we'll delve into the art of bouncing back from setbacks — a skill that transforms stumbling blocks into stepping stones on your path to success.

Cultivating Resilience and Mental Toughness

Resilience is the invisible armor that shields us from the impact of setbacks. It's the unwavering belief that no matter how tough the challenge, we have the strength to overcome it. Think of it as the muscle that grows stronger with each trial. But how can you cultivate this resilience, this mental fortitude that enables you to weather storms and emerge unscathed?

First, acknowledge that setbacks are not indicators of your worth, but rather opportunities for growth. They're the teachers that show us where we need to strengthen our strategies and our mindset. It's crucial to practice self-compassion during setbacks, recognizing that mistakes are stepping stones toward wisdom. Just as a tree bends but doesn't break in the wind, cultivating resilience means facing adversity with an open heart and a steadfast spirit.

Surround yourself with a support network that bolsters your resilience. Seek out mentors, friends, or groups that understand the journey you're on and can provide insights or a lending ear during challenging times. The process of bouncing back becomes easier when you're not navigating it alone.

Learning and Adapting from Past Failures

Failures are rarely final; they're the stepping stones to success. Each setback holds within it a valuable lesson, a piece of the puzzle that, when deciphered, can illuminate your path forward. Look at every stumble as an opportunity to learn and adapt. What went wrong? What could you have done differently? How can you adjust your approach moving forward?

Remember that failure isn't a reflection of your potential; it's a snapshot in time. It's a single chapter in your story, not the entire book. When you approach setbacks as lessons, they lose their power to hold you back. They become catalysts for evolution, refining your strategies and forging your character.

Transforming Setbacks into Springboards

One of the most remarkable powers you possess is the ability to transform setbacks into springboards. Picture a trampoline: the harder you fall, the higher it propels you. Similarly, setbacks can launch you toward greater heights when you harness their energy. This transformation begins with your mindset. Instead of dwelling on what went wrong, focus on what you can learn from the experience.

Every setback is a chance to reevaluate your goals and redefine your strategies. It's an opportunity to pivot, adapt, and approach your dreams from a new angle. When you view setbacks as integral parts of your journey rather than roadblocks, you tap into a wellspring of resilience and creativity.

A setback can also serve as a reminder of your commitment. When you overcome adversity, you reinforce your dedication to your dreams. You demonstrate that your passion is unbreakable and your determination unwavering. The strength you cultivate in the face of setbacks becomes an essential part of your narrative, shaping not only your journey but also inspiring others on their paths.

Setbacks are threads woven alongside victories, dreams, and aspirations. They're the challenges that reveal your character, the opportunities that define your journey. Through resilience, learning, and transformation, you can navigate setbacks with grace and emerge stronger than ever. Remember, setbacks are not the end; they're the beginning of a new chapter, one that propels you forward with a renewed sense of purpose and unwavering determination.

The Role of Patience and Perseverance

Life is a journey paved with twists and turns, peaks and valleys, and dreams that dance between setbacks and successes. In the heart of this dynamic journey lies a duo that holds unparalleled power: patience and perseverance. Imagine them as your trusted guides, leading you through the labyrinth of challenges, towards the fulfillment of your dreams.

The Virtue of Patience in Dream Achievement

Patience, often described as a virtue, is a beacon of calm in a world fueled by haste. It's the ability to hold space for your dreams to unfurl in their own time, recognizing that the most beautiful flowers bloom gradually, under the tender care of time itself. When pursuing your dreams, patience is not a passive act; it's a conscious choice to trust the process and believe in the divine timing of things.

Dreams rarely unfold with the snap of a finger. They evolve through dedication, learning, and continuous effort. Patience doesn't mean idly waiting; rather, it's about nurturing your dreams with unwavering faith and nurturing each step of progress. It's understanding that setbacks and challenges are integral to growth, and they provide opportunities to learn and adjust your course.

As you navigate the intricate path to your dreams, remind yourself that the journey is as important as the destination. Embrace each moment with a patient heart, knowing that even though the road might be winding, every step you take brings you closer to the realization of your aspirations.

Staying Steadfast Amidst Delayed Gratification
In an era of instant gratification, where a swipe or a click can bring us what we desire, the art of delayed gratification stands as a testament to your commitment to your dreams. It's about embracing the long game, understanding that the sweetest victories often require time to mature. As you chase your dreams, remember that the journey of achievement is not a sprint but a marathon.

Delayed gratification instills discipline and resilience, allowing you to withstand the allure of quick fixes that might lead you astray from your true path. It's about focusing on the big picture while savoring the small wins along the way. Each step forward, no matter how small, is a triumph that contributes to the grand narrative of your dream story.

During moments when instant results seem enticing, remind yourself of the magic that comes from patiently tending to your dreams. The growth that occurs through steady effort is a testament to your dedication, proving that the journey is worth every ounce of patience invested.

Trusting the Process While Aiming for Progress
In the intricate dance between patience and progress, it's vital to maintain a balance that cultivates growth while acknowledging the importance of waiting. Trusting the process doesn't mean relinquishing control; rather, it's about finding harmony between doing and being, between striving and surrendering.

Imagine building a puzzle. Each piece contributes to the whole, but it takes time and attention to fit them together seamlessly. Similarly, your dreams are like pieces of a puzzle waiting to be aligned. Every setback, every lesson learned, and every moment of patience contributes to the puzzle of your dream's realization.

As you trust the process, remember to celebrate progress, no matter how small it might seem. Acknowledge your achievements, reflect on the lessons learned, and embrace the growth you've experienced. This sense of progress fuels your perseverance and reaffirms your belief that every step you take, no matter how incremental, is a step closer to the summit of your dreams.

Patience and perseverance are the support that holding resilience into your journey. They are your allies during challenging times, your companions during plateaus, and your guiding lights when the path ahead seems uncertain. Embrace patience as a beacon of hope, delayed gratification as a testament to your dedication, and trust in the process as your constant companion on the path to dream fulfillment.

Chapter 15: Reflection and Renewal

Harnessing the Power of Reflection

In the whirlwind of life, it's all too easy to get caught up in the momentum of our dreams, relentlessly charging forward without looking back. Yet, there is a moment of pause, a powerful act that can transform the trajectory of our journey – reflection. In this sub-chapter, we'll explore how harnessing the power of reflection can be the compass guiding us toward dream fulfillment and instrument for propelling us forward.

Regularly Assessing Goals and Progress

Imagine your dreams as constellations in the night sky, guiding your way through the vast expanse of possibilities. Regularly assessing your goals and progress is akin to taking a celestial navigation of your aspirations. It's about taking a deliberate step back from the rush, allowing yourself the space to evaluate how far you've come and where you're headed.

Regular assessment doesn't mean constant self-critique; it's a practice of gentle observation and honest acknowledgment. It's a time to celebrate the milestones you've reached, the challenges you've conquered, and the growth you've experienced. This process not only keeps you connected to your dreams but also fuels your motivation as you witness the tangible impact of your efforts.

The act of regular assessment also serves as a compass for fine-tuning your course. Just as a sailor adjusts the sails to catch the wind, you adjust your strategies to align with your changing circumstances. Perhaps you've encountered unexpected opportunities that have reshaped your path. By reflecting on your goals and progress, you equip yourself with the insights needed to recalibrate and navigate even more effectively toward your dreams.

Insights Gained from Introspection

Consider introspection as the lantern you carry into the depths of your being, illuminating the hidden corners of your thoughts, emotions, and motivations. It's the art of self-inquiry, a practice that requires stillness and curiosity. When you embrace introspection, you invite yourself into a rich dialogue with your inner world.

Introspection is not about dwelling on the past or dwelling on what could have been. It's about exploring the present moment with a sense of curiosity, uncovering the patterns that shape your behaviors and decisions. What fears hold you back? What passions drive you forward? What beliefs influence your choices? These questions form the foundation of introspection.

Through introspection, you gain insights that lead to profound self-awareness. You identify recurring themes, both empowering and limiting, that impact your journey. You discover the roots of your motivations and the sources of your doubts. Armed with these insights, you can intentionally nurture the aspects that empower you and actively work on transforming those that hinder your progress.

Adjusting Dreams to Align with Evolving Desires

As you journey through life, your dreams are not static destinations; they evolve alongside you. Think of your dreams as living entities that respond to the changes in your experiences, values, and aspirations. This is where the art of adjusting dreams comes into play – a process that harmonizes your evolving desires with your pursuit of fulfillment.

Just as a gardener tends to their plants, you tend to your dreams by regularly assessing whether they still resonate with your true self. As you grow, your perspective shifts, and what once captivated your heart might evolve into something even more profound. By adjusting your dreams, you align your journey with your authentic desires, ensuring that your efforts are directed toward pursuits that bring you the utmost fulfillment.

Adjusting dreams doesn't mean abandoning them. It's about honoring the growth you've undergone and the wisdom you've gained. It's the understanding that your journey is a canvas, and as you paint your story, you're allowed to change the strokes and hues. This flexibility ensures that your path remains authentic, allowing you to move forward with clarity and purpose.

In the adventure of life, reflection is the grand mirror to look into wisdom. Through regular assessment, introspection, and the adjustment of dreams, you create a symphony of insight that guides you toward a more aligned and fulfilling existence. So, as you journey forward, remember to pause and look back, for in the echoes of your past, you'll find the keys to unlocking a brighter future.

The Importance of Recharging and Renewal

In the bustling mosaic of life, where dreams are woven and aspirations take flight, there's a rhythm that's easy to overlook. It's the gentle ebb and flow that carries us through challenges and triumphs, and it's essential for maintaining the vitality required to chase our dreams. We're about to explore a vital chapter in the story of achieving dreams – a chapter that's often underestimated but holds the key to sustained success and well-being: the art of recharging and renewal.

Avoiding Burnout and Overexertion

Picture this: a candle burning at both ends, casting a brilliant light that gradually dims until it sputters out. This image is a reflection of what can happen when we neglect the signs of burnout and overexertion. In the pursuit of dreams, it's easy to fall into the trap of pushing ourselves beyond our limits, believing that unrelenting effort is the only path to success.

However, consider this alternative perspective: by recognizing the importance of self-care and balance, we can actually enhance our chances of reaching our goals. Burnout not only affects our physical and mental well-being but can also lead to a deterioration in the quality of our work. It's the equivalent of depleting the very energy we need to fuel our aspirations.

To avoid burnout, we must learn to listen to our bodies and minds. Rest is not a sign of weakness; it's a prerequisite for sustainable achievement. By setting healthy boundaries, prioritizing sleep, and allowing ourselves breaks, we recharge our batteries and ensure that we're always operating at our best. Remember, it's not the speed at which we run that matters, but the endurance to finish the race.

Methods for Rejuvenating Creativity and Energy
Creativity is the heartbeat of progress, and energy is the life force that sustains it. Yet, even the most vibrant wellspring can run dry without proper care. In this segment, we'll explore methods to replenish creativity and energy, infusing them with renewed vitality.

One potent method is stepping away from the familiar. Engaging in new experiences, whether it's exploring a different environment or learning a new skill, stimulates our minds and breathes fresh life into our perspectives. Remember, innovation often arises at the intersection of seemingly unrelated ideas.

Physical well-being is also an integral part of sustaining energy and creativity. Regular exercise, a balanced diet, and adequate hydration fortify our bodies, enabling us to weather the demands of our pursuits. These seemingly mundane practices ripple through our work, enhancing our clarity of thought and our capacity to generate original ideas.

The Art of Embracing Downtime for Future Success
In a world that celebrates productivity, downtime might appear as wasted moments. But here's the truth: downtime is an investment in our future success. It's the space in which our minds rejuvenate, our ideas germinate, and our spirits recharge. By intentionally carving out time for rest, we lay the foundation for sustained achievement.

Think of downtime as fertile soil. When we plant the seeds of relaxation and contemplation, we create a breeding ground for inspiration to flourish. This might involve immersing yourself in hobbies, spending quality time with loved ones, or simply engaging in quiet reflection. These seemingly leisurely activities nourish our souls, enabling us to return to our endeavors with increased focus and vigor.

Rest is not a sign of weakness; it's a testament to your wisdom. By embracing the art of recharging and renewal, you embark on a journey of holistic success. You create a narrative where achievement is not a frantic race, but a rhythmic dance of balance. So, dare to pause, to breathe, and to nurture the very wellspring that fuels your dreams. In this sacred space of renewal, you'll discover the secret to sustainable success.

Rekindling Passion and Purpose

Life is an ever-evolving journey, marked by moments of triumph, introspection, and transformation. As we traverse this path, our dreams often take center stage, propelling us forward with unwavering determination. Yet, there are moments when the fire that once burned so brightly within us might flicker, or even seem to dim. This is a natural part of the journey, and it's during these times that we must embark on a quest to rekindle our passion and purpose.

Rediscovering the Initial Spark of Dreams

Close your eyes for a moment and think back to the very beginning of your journey. Can you recall the sensation of excitement, the uncontainable energy that surged through you when you first dared to dream? That initial spark, the moment of clarity when you envisioned your dreams, is an invaluable treasure. It's a beacon that can guide you back to the heart of what matters most to you.

Rediscovering that spark involves revisiting the core reasons behind your dreams. What fueled your desire to achieve them in the first place? Was it a burning need to make a difference, a deep longing for personal growth, or an insatiable thirst for adventure? By delving into these roots, you can reignite the passion that once set you on this path.

Sometimes, the demands of daily life can cast a shadow over our dreams. But remember, just because a fire dims doesn't mean it's extinguished. It's waiting for you to breathe life into it once more. Spend time reflecting on the moments that inspired you, the challenges that tested you, and the victories that affirmed your journey. By reconnecting with these memories, you'll find the embers of your passion ready to blaze anew.

Finding New Avenues for Inspiration
Passion and inspiration are intertwined in a dance that never truly ends. Life's landscape is rich with avenues that can spark your imagination and reignite your creative energy. Often, all it takes is a shift in perspective to open your eyes to a world of new possibilities.

Explore realms outside your comfort zone. Dive into literature, art, music, or nature – sources of boundless inspiration. Engaging with new experiences awakens your senses and encourages your mind to break free from its routine. A single moment, a fleeting interaction, or a breathtaking view can serve as a catalyst for renewed enthusiasm.

Furthermore, seek out role models and stories of those who've overcome obstacles to achieve their dreams. Their journeys can offer fresh perspectives and ignite a sense of camaraderie. Remember, inspiration isn't confined to grand gestures; it can be found in the everyday lives of those who embody dedication and resilience.

Fusing Passion and Purpose for Lasting Fulfillment
Passion and purpose are like intertwined threads, weaving through the fabric of your dreams. Passion is the fervent emotion that propels you forward, while purpose provides the deeper meaning that anchors your efforts. When you fuse these elements, you create a powerful force that propels you toward lasting fulfillment.

To align passion and purpose, begin by revisiting your dreams with a discerning eye. What facets of your journey resonate most strongly with your values and aspirations? What impact do you wish to make on the world around you? Aligning your dreams with a higher purpose enhances their significance and fuels your dedication.

As you pursue your dreams, regularly reassess their alignment with your evolving values and vision. Allow room for adaptation while staying true to the essence that ignites your passion. This balance between adaptability and authenticity fosters a sustainable sense of purpose.

In the journey of life, the chapter of rekindling passion and purpose is one of depth and significance. It's a chapter where you fan the flames of your inner fire, emboldening your journey with renewed enthusiasm. By rediscovering that initial spark, embracing new sources of inspiration, and fusing passion with purpose, you breathe new life into your dreams. As you continue to evolve, so too will your dreams, reflecting the wondrous journey of growth and fulfillment you've embarked upon.

Chapter 16: Celebrating Dream Achievement

Acknowledging Milestones and Progress

In the journey toward our dreams, there's an often overlooked but incredibly powerful practice: acknowledging the small wins along the way. These little victories, like hidden gems on a path, play a pivotal role in our overall success. They are the building blocks of our achievements, the subtle strokes that shape our masterpiece. In this sub-chapter, we'll delve into the profound significance of recognizing these milestones, how it cultivates a positive mindset, and why these achievements can serve as a wellspring of motivation for our future dreams.

The Value of Recognizing Small Wins

Imagine a painter meticulously crafting a work of art. Each brushstroke contributes to the whole, and each detail adds depth and richness. Similarly, every step we take toward our dreams, no matter how small, contributes to the museum of our success story. Recognizing these smaller milestones is like taking a step back from the canvas to admire the intricate strokes that make up the bigger picture.

Why is this recognition so crucial? Because it's easy to get caught up in the grandeur of our end goals, the mountains we aim to conquer. Yet, by solely focusing on the summit, we risk missing the beautiful scenery along the way. Acknowledging small wins allows us to fully appreciate the journey, boosting our morale and infusing each step with a sense of purpose.

Furthermore, celebrating small achievements provides us with tangible evidence of progress. It's a reminder that we're moving forward, even if it's just a single step at a time. This accumulation of small successes bolsters our confidence and fuels our belief that we're capable of achieving even greater feats.

Cultivating a Positive Mindset Through Celebration
Celebration isn't just a spontaneous burst of joy; it's a conscious choice to embrace positivity and gratitude. When we take the time to celebrate our achievements, no matter how modest, we actively cultivate a positive mindset. It's like nurturing a garden of optimism in the fertile soil of our thoughts.

Think about it: as you celebrate your small wins, you're directing your focus toward the positives in your life. This shift in perspective has a profound impact on your mental and emotional well-being. It's like reprogramming your brain to scan for the good stuff rather than fixating on what's lacking or challenging.

Moreover, celebrating small wins enhances our resilience. Life's journey is filled with ups and downs, but by fostering a positive mindset, we equip ourselves with a buoyant attitude that helps us weather storms with grace. It's like building an emotional shield that deflects negativity and nurtures our mental fortitude.

Using Achievements as Motivation for Future Dreams
Have you ever noticed that accomplishing a goal often
ignites a hunger for more? It's because success breeds
success. When we achieve even the smallest of dreams, we
awaken an insatiable appetite for more achievement. These
accomplishments become like milestones on a road map,
guiding us toward the grander visions we hold for our lives.

By celebrating small wins and using them as stepping
stones, we're essentially creating a staircase to our future
dreams. Each achievement paves the way for the next,
giving us the confidence and momentum to tackle bigger
challenges. It's a process of building upon our
accomplishments, layer by layer, until we stand atop a
mountain of achievements that once felt distant and
unattainable.

Furthermore, these achievements serve as tangible
reminders of our capabilities. When we encounter obstacles
on the path to our dreams, we can look back at what we've
achieved and draw strength from those victories. We can
tell ourselves, "If I did that, I can overcome this." It's a well
of motivation that never runs dry, fueling us to persistently
chase after our most audacious dreams.

Acknowledging small wins is a practice of profound
significance. It's a testament to the progress we've made, an
affirmation of our positive mindset, and a wellspring of
motivation for the dreams that still await us. As you
journey toward your aspirations, remember that every step

counts, every achievement matters, and every celebration is
a testament to your unstoppable spirit.

Embracing the Journey of Dream Fulfillment

Imagine standing on the peak of a mountain, gazing at the
breathtaking view below. The journey that brought you
here wasn't merely a collection of steps; it was an odyssey
that transformed you in ways you never thought possible.
As you bask in the glory of your dream's realization, you're
not just celebrating an endpoint; you're celebrating the
entire voyage. Welcome to the chapter of your life where
you learn to embrace the journey of dream fulfillment.

Reflecting on the Transformational Journey

Close your eyes for a moment and take a mental leap back
to where it all began. Picture the initial spark that ignited
your dream — that moment of inspiration that set your
heart racing with excitement. Reflecting on this
transformational journey means retracing the path that took
you from that initial spark to where you stand today. It's
about acknowledging the growth, the setbacks, and the
small victories that led you to this point.

Each step, each choice, and each challenge played a pivotal
role in sculpting you into the person you've become. The
journey might have been winding, with unexpected twists
and turns, but every detour offered lessons that were
essential for your development. Remember, it's not just

about reaching the destination; it's about the experiences that shaped you along the way.

Extracting Lessons and Wisdom from the Process
In the intricate of your dream journey, every thread is a lesson waiting to be unraveled. As you stand at this milestone, it's time to gently pull at those threads and extract the wisdom they hold. What did you learn about yourself? What skills did you acquire? What fears did you conquer? These insights aren't just for your personal growth; they're also valuable gifts you can share with others who are on their own journey.

Extracting lessons and wisdom from the process is about uncovering the pearls of knowledge that might have gone unnoticed amidst the hustle. It's about recognizing patterns, making connections, and uncovering the underlying threads that guided your progress. Sometimes, the most profound lessons come from the challenges you faced, offering you a chance to discover strengths you never knew you had.

Nurturing Gratitude for Every Step Taken
Gratitude is the heartbeat of your journey — a melody that resonates through every step, every triumph, and even every stumble. As you celebrate your dream's realization, it's important to pause and nurture gratitude for every single step taken. Gratitude isn't just about acknowledging the big wins; it's about finding joy in the mundane, the small victories, and even the moments of struggle.

Nurturing gratitude amplifies the sense of fulfillment you experience. It's a practice that keeps you grounded and reminds you of the progress you've made. It's about appreciating the people who supported you, the opportunities that arose, and the growth that came from challenges. When you approach your journey with a heart full of gratitude, you infuse your celebrations with a deeper sense of meaning.

In this celebration of dream fulfillment, it's not just about the destination. It's about the transformation you underwent, the lessons you learned, and the gratitude you nurtured. As you stand on this peak, take a moment to marvel at the beauty of the path you've walked. Your journey is a testament to your strength, your resilience, and your unwavering commitment to realizing your dreams.

The journey doesn't end here; it continues, enriched by the experiences you've collected. As you move forward, let the reflections, the lessons, and the gratitude be your compass. Embrace your journey, for it's the journey that shapes you into the dream achiever you've become.

Sharing Your Success Story

Imagine standing at the peak of a mountain, the wind carrying whispers of accomplishment. As you look back on your journey, you realize that your path was not just about personal triumph—it was about leaving a trail for others to follow. Welcome to the chapter of celebration where sharing your success story becomes a beacon of light for fellow dreamers.

Inspiring Others Through Your Journey
Your journey, unique as it is, holds within it a painting of experiences, setbacks, and breakthroughs. By sharing this journey, you have the power to ignite sparks of inspiration in the hearts of others. When you share your struggles and how you overcame them, you become a living testament that dreams are attainable, even in the face of adversity.

Consider this: your challenges, once surmounted, become stepping stones for someone else. When you share how you turned setbacks into opportunities, you offer a roadmap for others navigating similar terrain. Your story serves as a reminder that resilience, persistence, and the power of belief can move mountains.

Every triumph you celebrate is an opportunity to pass the torch of motivation. Your journey, like a candle's flame, can light the way for others who are venturing into the shadows of doubt. As you recount your experiences, do so with an open heart and a sincere desire to uplift those who yearn to follow in your footsteps.

Effective Storytelling for Maximum Impact
In the realm of sharing your success story, storytelling emerges as the hero. Storytelling is the art of draw words into a painting that captivates, engages, and resonates with

your audience. It's not just about the facts; it's about conveying emotions, experiences, and life lessons through narrative.

To tell your story effectively, start by connecting with the emotions that defined your journey. What were the moments of triumph, the instances of doubt, and the turning points that guided you? Craft a narrative that takes your audience on a journey—a journey that mirrors the twists and turns of your own.

Vivid details and relatable anecdotes can transform your story into a vivid landscape in the minds of your listeners. By sharing your vulnerabilities, you invite others to connect with you on a human level. They'll see themselves in your struggles and victories, creating a sense of shared experience that's both powerful and uplifting.

Paying It Forward by Helping Others Chase Dreams
As you celebrate your dream achievements, the spotlight isn't just on you—it's also on the impact you can create in the lives of others. Paying it forward becomes an integral part of the celebration. Your journey, once shared, can be the catalyst that propels others toward their dreams.

Paying it forward involves more than just sharing your story; it's about actively helping others chase their dreams. It's offering guidance, insights, and support to individuals who are on their own paths of aspiration. This could be through mentoring, workshops, or even through simple acts of encouragement.

When you help others chase their dreams, you create a ripple effect of positive change. Their achievements become a continuation of your own legacy. Your success story, once told, transforms into a bridge that connects dreamers across time and space, united by the shared pursuit of possibility.

Sharing your success story isn't just a celebration of your accomplishments; it's a gift you bestow upon the world. By inspiring others, telling your story with impact, and paying it forward, you become a beacon of hope for those who dare to dream. Your journey becomes a part of the of human inspiration, a testament to the remarkable power of dreams realized.

Chapter 17: Sustaining Dream-Driven Living

The Continuous Cycle of Dreaming

In the journey of life, dreams are the compass that guides us, the stars that light our way. Yet, the beauty of dreams lies not only in their realization but in their perpetual evolution. Imagine a garden where the seeds of your dreams are sown, nurtured, and eventually transform into a lush forest of accomplishments. This is the essence of the continuous cycle of dreaming – a journey that transcends mere achievement and becomes a way of life.

Embracing Lifelong Learning and Growth

In journey of your life, the quest for dreams is intricately woven with the threads of learning and growth. The desire to achieve our dreams naturally propels us toward new horizons, new skills, and new knowledge. But here's the secret: the journey itself is as important as the destination.

Lifelong learning is the fuel that keeps the fire of your dreams burning brightly. It's about seeking knowledge not just for the sake of achieving a specific goal, but for the sheer joy of expanding your understanding of the world. With each piece of knowledge gained, you broaden your perspective, refine your skills, and elevate your capacity to dream bigger.

Consider this: as you gather new insights and experiences, your dreams may take unexpected turns. Lifelong learning enables you to adapt to these twists, embracing change with enthusiasm rather than resistance. It's a powerful reminder that growth isn't just a destination; it's a journey that enriches every aspect of your life.

Evolving Dreams as Life Changes

Life is an ever-changing landscape, and your dreams should be no different. Like a river that meanders through diverse terrain, your dreams have the flexibility to evolve alongside your experiences and circumstances. Embracing the ebb and flow of life allows your dreams to remain relevant and meaningful, even in the face of change.

Evolving dreams isn't about abandoning your initial aspirations; it's about refining and expanding them. As you progress through life, your priorities may shift, and new passions may arise. This natural evolution doesn't diminish the significance of your past dreams; instead, it adds layers of depth to your journey.

Imagine this as a canvas that you keep painting upon, adding new strokes and colors to create a masterpiece that tells the story of your life. This evolution empowers you to align your dreams with your current values, aspirations, and the person you've become. By allowing your dreams to grow with you, you ensure that they remain a source of inspiration and fulfillment.

Dreaming Beyond Individual Achievements

The essence of the continuous cycle of dreaming lies in understanding that dreams aren't confined to individual achievements. While personal aspirations are indeed significant, they are just the beginning. Dreams have the power to transcend the realm of the individual and contribute to a larger narrative of positive change.

Consider how your dreams can ripple outward, impacting not only your life but also the lives of others and the community you're a part of. Your dreams can inspire, motivate, and catalyze others to pursue their own aspirations. This interconnectedness creates a beautiful painting of shared dreams that draw a more vibrant and harmonious world.

Dreaming beyond individual achievements means aligning your aspirations with a greater purpose. It's about considering how your dreams can serve the greater good, leaving a lasting legacy that extends beyond your lifetime. This perspective infuses your journey with a sense of fulfillment that goes beyond personal success.

As you embrace lifelong learning, adapt your dreams to life's changes, and envision a future beyond yourself, you become a custodian of possibility. Remember, the journey is not confined to the mountaintop but is enriched by the trails you traverse along the way. In this cycle, dreams are not just destinations; they are the threads that weave the story of a life lived fully, purposefully, and passionately.

Leaving a Legacy of Dreamers

In the symphony of life, the most beautiful melodies are often those that reverberate long after the music stops. Imagine your life as a song, with each note representing a dream realized, a goal achieved, and a positive impact made. Now, imagine the ripple effect of that song, as it inspires others to compose their own melodies and chase their dreams with fervor. This is the essence of leaving a legacy of dreamers—a legacy that transcends individual accomplishments and extends into the realm of collective inspiration.

Empowering Others to Pursue Their Dreams

Picture this: a world in which each person possesses the tools, confidence, and motivation to pursue their dreams. This vision is not only attainable but also within your grasp to help shape. Empowering others to pursue their dreams is a gift that keeps giving, an investment that appreciates over time. It's about guiding others to recognize their potential, overcome obstacles, and chart their course to success.

Empowerment begins with active encouragement. By being a source of unwavering support, you create an environment in which others feel safe to express their aspirations. Offer a listening ear, share your own experiences, and offer practical advice when sought. As you do so, you provide a lifeline for dreamers navigating uncharted waters, reminding them that they're not alone on this journey.

Mentorship, too, plays a pivotal role in empowerment. By sharing your knowledge, insights, and wisdom, you pave the way for others to learn from your experiences. It's a symbiotic relationship—a dance of exchange in which both mentor and mentee grow and evolve. By nurturing a mindset of continuous learning and curiosity, you foster a generation of dreamers equipped to face the challenges that lie ahead.

Cultivating a Legacy of Positive Impact
In the orchestra of life, the song of your actions pave a legacy that resonates through time. The impact you make extends far beyond the boundaries of your lifetime, influencing generations to come. Cultivating a legacy of positive impact is about being mindful of the footprints you leave, making intentional choices that create a ripple effect of positivity.

Your legacy is shaped not only by your successes but also by your character and values. It's about integrity, compassion, and empathy. Every act of kindness, no matter how small, contributes to the legacy you're building. By embodying the qualities you wish to see in the world, you become a beacon of inspiration for others to follow suit.

Consider the power of leading by example. When you demonstrate resilience in the face of challenges, determination in pursuit of dreams, and kindness in your interactions, you set a standard for others to emulate. Your actions send a message that resonates far beyond words, showing that dreams are attainable and that positive impact is within everyone's reach.

Fostering a Community of Dream-Driven Individuals
Collaboration creates harmonies that are simply unattainable in isolation. Fostering a community of dream-driven individuals is about recognizing the strength in unity, about acknowledging that dreams shared become dreams multiplied. It's the recognition that we're stronger together, that our collective energy can propel us toward new horizons.

A dream-driven community is built on a foundation of support, encouragement, and shared aspirations. It's a space where individuals uplift each other, celebrate successes, and offer solace during challenges. By contributing your energy to such a community, you contribute to an ecosystem where dreams flourish and where collaboration sparks innovation.

Community-building involves creating spaces for dialogue and connection. It might be a physical gathering, a virtual platform, or even a simple group chat. It's about nurturing an environment in which dreamers can exchange ideas, seek advice, and find inspiration. As you foster connections, you'll witness the magic that happens when dream-driven individuals unite.

In the grand symphony of life, leaving a legacy of dreamers is a composition that transcends time. It's about empowering others to realize their potential, cultivating a legacy of positive impact, and fostering a community of individuals who chase their dreams relentlessly. As you weave your story into the fabric of this legacy, remember that your influence extends far beyond yourself. You're a conductor of inspiration, a composer of possibility, and a guiding light for generations of dreamers yet to come.

The Everlasting Quest for Fulfillment

Imagine life as a grand adventure, an uncharted journey filled with dreams, ambitions, and aspirations that stretch as far as the eye can see. Yet, within this vast landscape, there's a destination that transcends all others — a place where the heart finds solace, where purpose blooms, and where the pursuit of dreams converges with the quest for fulfillment. Welcome to the realm of everlasting fulfillment, a journey that embraces the dynamic dance between contentment and perpetual aspiration.

The Dynamic Nature of Fulfillment

Fulfillment is a state of being that often seems elusive, like chasing after a mirage in the desert of life. Just when we think we've grasped it, it slips through our fingers, leaving us yearning for more. The truth is, fulfillment isn't a stagnant oasis; it's a dynamic river that flows with the currents of our experiences and emotions.

This river of fulfillment is fueled by a sense of accomplishment, connection, and purpose. It's the feeling you get when you see the seeds of your dreams sprouting into reality. It's the warmth of sharing your achievements with loved ones. It's the alignment of your actions with your core values. Yet, as your dreams evolve and your horizons expand, so does the river of fulfillment. It's a perpetual journey of growth and transformation, where new dreams replace old ones and the pursuit of purpose continues to evolve.

Balancing Contentment with Continuous Aspiration
Contentment and aspiration are harmony that weave together in a delicate dance. Contentment is the gentle breeze that whispers, "You are enough as you are." It's the art of savoring the present moment, of finding joy in simple pleasures, and of appreciating the progress you've made. Contentment is the foundation upon which you build the framework of your dreams, a reminder that your worth isn't solely determined by your accomplishments.

On the other hand, continuous aspiration is the fuel that propels you forward, the fire that ignites new possibilities. It's the energy that stirs within you, urging you to reach for the stars, to explore uncharted territories, and to dream bigger than ever before. Aspiration is the catalyst that fuels your growth, pushing you beyond your comfort zone and into the realm of the unknown. It's the acknowledgment that there's always room for improvement, for expansion, and for the pursuit of new dreams.

Finding the equilibrium between contentment and aspiration is an art that requires self-awareness and mindfulness. It's about recognizing when to bask in the glow of your achievements and when to set your sights on new horizons. It's a delicate balance that allows you to cherish what you have while fueling your appetite for what's to come.

Embracing a Lifetime of Purpose-Driven Living

As you embark on the journey of dream-driven living, you weave the threads of purpose into the very fabric of your being. Purpose is the compass that guides you through the twists and turns of life, steering you toward the true north of your dreams. It's the force that propels you out of bed in the morning, infusing each day with intention and meaning.

A purpose-driven life is not just about achieving individual goals; it's about contributing to something greater than yourself. It's about leaving a legacy of impact and inspiration for those who come after you. It's the understanding that your dreams are interconnected with the dreams of others, that the painting of existence is draw from line of shared purpose.

Embracing a lifetime of purpose-driven living requires a commitment to continuous growth, to adaptability, and to the pursuit of dreams that align with your evolving self. It's the embodiment of a philosophy that recognizes that the journey itself is as valuable as the destination. It's a mindset that embraces the ebb and flow of fulfillment, the delicate balance between contentment and aspiration, and the realization that the quest for purpose is an ongoing adventure that transcends the boundaries of time.

As you navigate the ever-evolving landscape of dream-driven living, remember that fulfillment is not a static destination; it's a journey that unfolds with each step you take. Embrace the dynamic nature of your aspirations, find harmony between contentment and the pursuit of more, and live each day with purpose as your guiding light. In doing so, you'll embark on a lifelong odyssey of fulfillment, leaving footprints of inspiration and joy along the path you tread.

Epilogue: Embracing the Journey, Enriching Life's Canvas

And so, dear reader, as you approach the final chapters of this transformative expedition, take a moment to pause, reflect, and appreciate the intricate web of insights and wisdom you've woven into the fabric of your life. The voyage you've embarked upon, the pages you've turned, and the lessons you've absorbed have become the threads that artfully shape the narrative of your dreams.

As you contemplate the chapters that have unfolded, remember that this voyage was never about reaching a static destination. Instead, it's been about embracing the dynamic rhythm of dreams, aspirations, and the pursuit of fulfillment. The path you've traversed has been as much about the process as it has been about the outcomes, as much about growth as it has been about accomplishments.

Within these pages, you've unearthed that the pursuit of dreams is a complex symphony of growth, setbacks, triumphs, and even more growth. The concept of fulfillment has shifted from a distant horizon to an internal river that courses within you—a current that propels you ahead through life's various seasons.

You've adeptly navigated the delicate equilibrium between contentment and aspiration, recognizing that both hold their rightful place in the canvas of your existence. Contentment invites you to bask in the warmth of the present moment, celebrating your progress and finding delight in life's simplest pleasures. Aspiration, on the other hand, propels you into uncharted territories, encouraging you to dream bigger, delve deeper, and leave an enduring mark that stretches beyond your own journey.

Amid the narrative of your dreams, you've interwoven threads of connection, collaboration, and community. The individuals you've encountered along the way have transformed from mere acquaintances to kindred spirits— fellow dreamers, co-authors of your tale, and companions on the quest for a purposeful existence. Through networking, effective communication, and shared values, you've constructed bridges that span beyond the limits of individual dreams.

As you stand on the brink of concluding this chapter, you've evolved into a steward of purpose, a harbinger of dreams. The purpose-driven life you've embraced isn't solely for personal gratification; it's an endeavor that bequeaths an inheritance of inspiration and positive influence for the generations to come. You've realized that the pursuit of dreams isn't a solitary endeavor; it's a collective symphony of aspirations that intertwine, fashioning a world that's more vibrant and enriched.

And as you close this chapter and embark upon the boundless horizon of tomorrow, remember that this book marks not the end of your journey but a milestone—a guidepost, a catalyst—for the forthcoming chapters of your narrative. The insights you've gleaned, the lessons you've imbibed, and the perspectives you've embraced are the tools that will continue to illuminate your path as you journey onward. Allow them to serve as a compass that navigates you through uncertainties, a beacon that dispels shadows, and a roadmap that directs you toward your dreams.

As you bid farewell to this book and embrace the infinite expanses of the future, bear in mind that you are the author of your own story. You hold the power to sculpt your narrative, to dream with purpose, and to exist with intent. Greet each moment as an occasion to weave new threads into the rich tapestry of your life, enriching your journey and forging a legacy that defies the boundaries of time.

May your dreams be boundless, your purpose unwavering, and your expedition an ever-evolving mosaic of growth and contentment. As you step forth into the world armed with renewed perspective, understand that your narrative is still unfolding, your dreams are within grasp, and your journey brims with limitless potential.

Thank you for sharing this journey with me. Until our paths converge again, continue to dream, to aspire, and to craft the unique masterpiece of your extraordinary life.